P9-BYI-805

California   Oregon   Montana   New Mexico

Long before Lewis and Clark, the trails were there. Paths first beaten into the landscape by the hooves of migrating horses, buffalo and elk, and later widened by the Indians as they began to follow the animals across the land and build their cultures.

Today these trails exist as highways that bind this once-wild land into a nation. And for the twentieth-century traveler they can become both a state of mind and of nature as you travel with Ralph Moody past a thousand campfires, a hundred massacres, and between the graves of outlaws and heroes in the most comprehensive book ever written about the old trails west.

"This major book on trails gives the reader some understanding of all that varied, beautiful space between the Mississippi and the Pacific, and its place in the larger story of the world."
—*New York Times Book Review*

"Particularly stirring reading for the tourist to take along on a trip to any part of the West."
—*Library Journal*

Gateways to the Northwest:

The Old Trails West, Volume II

By RALPH MOODY

BALLANTINE BOOKS • NEW YORK

TO EDNA
my beloved trailmate

Copyright © 1963 by Ralph Moody

Library of Congress Catalog Card Number: 63-15093

SBN 345-24025-1-150

This edition published by arrangement with
Thomas Y. Crowell Company.

First Printing: September, 1974

Printed in the United States of America

Cartographer: Herbert Anthony

BALLANTINE BOOKS
A Division of Random House, Inc.
201 East 50th Street, New York, N.Y. 10022
Simultaneously published by
Ballantine Books, Ltd., Toronto Canada

MORE THAN half a century ago, I was water boy on a large cattle ranch. Our range was on the rolling prairies along the foothills of the Rockies in northern Colorado. In summer the cattle were allowed to scatter for a considerable distance, with four or five cowhands spread out to keep them from drifting too far. My job was to ride the circuit morning and afternoon, carrying any orders the foreman wanted to send the men, and supplying them with water from a dogskin bag slung to the back of my saddle.

When the herd had grazed northward nearly to the Wyoming line I discovered a set of deep-worn old wheel ruts. Having little to do that day, I followed the overgrown trail for several miles, wondering: Why is it out here on the prairie, seemingly leading from nowhere to nowhere? Who first broke this trail, and what reason did he have for doing it? Why did he go this way instead of some other, and where was he going? Why were so many wagons driven over a road that did not seem to lead anywhere, and what were they hauling that made such deep wheel ruts?

The next man on my circuit was Hank Bevin, an oldtime cowhand, probably well along in his sixties, so I asked him the same questions I had asked myself.

"Anglin' off towards the nor'west, betwixt the Laramie and Medicine Bow ranges?" he asked.

"I don't know about the ranges, but the tracks were

angling toward the foothills northwest, not in the direction of Cheyenne."

"Wouldn't be," he said. "Cheyenne's a railroad town, and there wasn't no railroads when them ruts was wore. What you stumbled onto was the trace of the old Overland Stagecoach Line. I recollect when it run clean through from Missouri to Californy. Main trail of the Overland followed the North Platte and Sweetwater, but Ben Holladay, he swung his stage line south'ard from Julesburg to pick up the Denver trade. This here's the way he went back north to get through the mountains at the end of the Medicine Bows."

"How did he know where to get through the mountains?" I asked. "There doesn't appear to be any break in them along here."

"No, but there's lots of old buffalo trails. Didn't ever you take note how the deepest buffalo and wild horse trails always leads by the easiest way to the nearest water, the best grass, and the lowest mountain passes? Remember that if you aim to be a cattleman, and it'll save you a heap of trouble. That's all Ben, or whoever laid out the old stage line, had to know. Like as not he followed the trail of buffalo headin' for grass on the west side of the range."

"I wonder how he happened to come through this way," I said.

"Didn't happen to; needed to," Hank told me, "else he'd had to go three, four hundred miles out of his way. Don't no man nor no wild critter wear a trail where he happens to go; only where he needs to go. Find where a trail changed course and you'll find where the need of them passing over it changed. It's all wrote down for them that can read, just like it is with a man. An old man's story is wrote in lines on his face; an old trail's story is wrote in lines on the face of the earth."

Ever since that day I have tried to find out as much as I could about the early trails—from oldtimers, from riding considerable portions of them while the old ruts were still traceable, and from reading—but my search has always been for the why: Why was this trail blazed in the first place, by whom, and what were the needs that changed its course? There are many excellent books available regarding the history of individual western trails and the more important events which took place upon them. The purpose of this book is not to provide a comprehensive history of any trail, but to tell the story, from origin to obliteration of the ancient character lines that once seamed the face of the American West.—R. M.

Contents

Gateways to the Northwest:

The Old Trails West
Volume II

The Original Pathfinders

THE HISTORY of the United States is replete with the names of famous pioneers and pathfinders who are credited with blazing the old trails of the old West. Yet few of them blazed a trail that had not been traveled for countless generations. It is probable that most of the more important western trails had been worn deep long before the first human foot was planted on the North American continent.

Some sixty million years ago, the western portion of the North American continent lay beneath the sea, and southern Arizona was a tropical swamp. Then the Sierra Nevada and Cascade mountains were heaved up, forming a great peninsula and leaving a shallow inland sea to the eastward. The sea was roughly four hundred miles wide and a thousand long, stretching from the Gulf of California to southern Idaho. When the mountains rose they blocked the course of rain clouds blown in from the Pacific, and the inland sea evaporated until its only remaining vestige is Great Salt Lake. During millions of years the evaporating moisture was blown eastward in rain clouds, watering lush forests and grasslands that covered the high plateaus of Arizona, New Mexico, eastern Utah, and western Colorado. When the evaporation was completed Nevada, western Utah, southeastern California, and western Arizona were left desolate salt-impregnated deserts, and the high plateaus became arid wastelands.

Long before the rising of the Sierra Nevada, the Rocky Mountains had formed a solid bulwark, robbing rain clouds borne by the prevailing westerly winds, and leaving the high, rolling plains that stretched five hundred miles to the eastward a semiarid wilderness. Thus, for millions of years before there was human habitation, the western half of the mountainous regions. But in the high altitudes snow fell deep in winter and the summer rains were abundant.

Since the summits of the Sierra Nevada and Cascade mountains are on the eastern side of the ranges, most of the water from melting snow and rainfall flows westward into the Pacific. What little flows to the east is swallowed by the parched sands of the Great American Desert. On the other hand, the Rocky Mountains and their satellites are drained to almost every point of the compass: to the northwest by tributaries of the Columbia, to the northeast and east by tributaries of the Missouri, to the south by the Rio Grande, and to the southwest by the Colorado and its various branches.

With the exception of the Rio Grande, all these great river systems rise in the vicinity of Yellowstone Colorado, has its source a few miles to the south, and National Park. The Green River, an extension of the drains the entire area between the Rocky and Wasatch mountains. The Clark's Fork and Snake tributaries of the Columbia River reach eastward toward the park as if it were a block of ice and they were the jaws of a great pair of tongs open to seize it. The headwaters of the Missouri River rise a hundred and fifty miles inside the jaws of the tongs, while its largest tributary, the Yellowstone, reaches out to touch the lower jaw just outside the southeastern corner of the park. There Two Ocean Creek flows sluggishly along a flat, heavily wooded plateau on the exact line of the Continental Divide. Its waters diverge in a swampy area to form Atlantic Creek and Pacific Creek, making it possible for a trout to swim from one ocean to the other. The water

the curving tong of Snake River turns abruptly northward through awesome Hell's Canyon, but a series of
grassy plateaus and valleys leads on to the northwest,
reaching the broad valley of the Columbia north of
Pendleton. This is the route by which the horses of
the Great Plains are believed to have traveled in leaving the continent.

Many ethnologists believe that, at about the time the
horses left, Asiatics, the ancestors of the Indians,
crossed the land bridge in the opposite direction and
eventually spread throughout the Western Hemisphere.
How these people migrated to the various areas of
North America can only be conjectured by the regions
in which different linguistic groups were originally discovered. It is, however, probable that, being hunters
and fishermen, they followed animal trails and watercourses in their dispersal throughout the newly discovered land. There can be little doubt that many who
settled on the Great Plains, and farther to the east,
followed horse trails from the Columbia River through
the break in the rampart of the Rockies, for long before
the white men came this route was known to the
Indians as the Big Medicine Trail.

As the Indians scattered throughout the area that is
now the United States, rivers became their highways,
whether they traveled afoot or by canoe, for streams
could be followed great distances with assurance that
the traveler would be able to find his way back to the
starting point. It is not probable that any Indian made
a continuous transcontinental journey. The Indians did,
however, have definite transcontinental routes, and are
known to have traveled great distances over them. The
routes lay across the country like a great cable, tightly
wound at the center, its eastern quarter frazzled into
innumerable cords and fibers, and its western half un-
wound into three widely separated strands. The main
cable, kinked and twisting, looped between Kansas City
and Cincinnati along the Missouri, Mississippi, and

Ohio rivers. By way of the Ohio, its chief branches—
the Tennessee, Cumberland, and Allegheny—and their
hundreds of tributaries, the entire region west of the
Appalachian and Allegheny mountains could be reached
by direct watercourses, as far south as Alabama and
northward into New York.

The old trails of the old West were influenced only
by the three strands that lay across the prairies, mountains, and deserts between Kansas City and the Pacific
Ocean. Two of these remained tightly wound as they
followed the course of the Missouri River between
Kansas City and Omaha. There they separated. One
continued far northward up the Missouri to its headwaters in the vicinity of Yellowstone Park, crossed the
Continental Divide, and descended to the Pacific by
way of the northern tong of the Columbia River. The
other was the Big Medicine Trail; its course lay westward along the Platte and Sweetwater rivers to the
Continental Divide at South Pass, across the Green
River Valley, along the Bear, and on to the Pacific by
way of the southern tong of the Columbia.

The third strand of the great cable looped far to the
south, and followed four separate watercourses to reach
the Pacific. From as far east as the Allegheny Mountains, the Indians could travel to the northern and
central Rockies by continuous and direct watercourses.
But to reach the southern Rockies by a continuous
water route they must travel far down the Mississippi,
then back to the northwest along the Arkansas River,
lengthening the direct distance by several hundred miles.
To avoid this long detour, they learned to follow the
Missouri to the point where it turns northward at
Kansas City, paddle up the Kansas River and its
tributary, the Smoky Hill, then portage thirty miles
overland to the Arkansas at the point where it makes
its great northern bend in central Kansas.

In all probability the Indians discovered this more
direct route because of buffalo and other animal trails

that skirted the rivers and led from one to another where the overland distance was shortest. In any event, the route continued westward along the Arkansas to the foothills of the Rockies, descended the Rio Grande to southern New Mexico, then turned westward along the Gila (pronounced Heela) River to the Colorado, a few miles above the Gulf of California. This southern strand of the cable was known as the Gila Route and, together with the Big Medicine Trail, became the main line of many old trails of the West.

THE TRAILS AND

	Gila Trail	El Camino Real	Old Spanish Trail	Santa Fe Trail
1538	Esteban looks for Seven Cities			
1539	Diaz follows Esteban			
1540	Coronado's march			
1542		Cabrillo sails California coast		
1577		Drake sails California coast		
1602		Vizcaíno sails California coast		
1686	Kino to Pimería Alta			
1768	Garcés to Pimería Alta			
1769		Portolá at San Francisco Bay		
1774	Anza reaches Pacific	Anza to Monterey		
1775	Anza's colonizing party			
1776		Anza founds San Francisco	Escalante expedition	
1778				
1792				
1804				
1810				
1812				McKnight to Santa Fe
1821				Becknell opens Santa Fe trade
1822				Wagon party on Cimarron Cutoff
1823				
1824	Patties trap Gila			

THEIR TIMES

Big Medicine Trail	Oregon Trail	California Trail	—and meanwhile	
			Henry VIII reigns in England	1538
			De Soto explores Florida	1539
			Henry VIII marries Anne of Cleves	1540
			Russians trap in Alaska	1542
			Search for Northwest Passage	1577
			First Englishman in New England	1602
			Connecticut Charter Oak incident	1686
			Methodist church in New World	1768
			Daniel Boone sees Kentucky	1769
			First Continental Congress	1774
			Revolutionary War	1775
			Declaration of Independence	1776
Cook at Nootka Sound			Franklin negotiates French treaty	1778
Gray finds Columbia R.			Cotton gin invented	1792
Lewis and Clark to Columbia R.			Jefferson re-elected President	1804
Hunt to Ft. Astoria			West Florida annexed	1810
Stuart's return to St. Louis			War with England	1812
			Missouri admitted to Union	1821
			Brazil gains independence	1822
Smith-Fitzpatrick trapping party			Monroe Doctrine	1823
			John Q. Adams elected President	1824

	Gila Trail	El Camino Real	Old Spanish Trail	Santa Fe Trail
1826			Smith looks for Buena Ventura	
1827			Smith to San Gabriel again	Ft. Leavenworth built
1829	E. Young traps Gila		Armijo cutoff route	Bent caravan
1830	E. Young reaches San Gabriel		Wolfskill-Yount trapping party	Bent and St. Vrain caravan
1832				
1833				
1834				Bent's Ft. built
1836				
1841–42				
1843				
1846	Kearny's march			Kearny takes Santa Fe
1847				
1848				
1849	Duval gold-rush party			
1858	Butterfield Mail started			
1860				
1861				
1862	Apache Pass Battle			
1869				
1880				First train to Santa Fe

Big Medicine Trail	Oregon Trail	California Trail	—and meanwhile	
			First U.S. locomotive	1826
			Barbed wire invented	1827
			Andrew Jackson inaugurated	1829
			Indian Removal Act	1830
	Wyeth, settlers to Oregon		Black Hawk War	1832
		Walker to San Francisco Bay	Steel plow introduced	1833
	Wyeth's 2nd trip	Carson traps Humboldt R.	McCormick reaper patented	1834
	Whitman mission		Battle of the Alamo	1836
	De Smet to Columbia R.	Bidwell party to California	W. H. Harrison inaugurated; died	1841–42
		Frémont to Sutter's Ft.	Mormons adopt polygamy	1843
		Donner tragedy	Mexican War	1846
		B. Young to Utah	Scott in Mexico	1847
		Mormon handcarts to Utah	Gold found in California	1848
			Minnesota becomes a Territory	1849
			First Atlantic-cable message	1858
		Pony Express	Lincoln elected	1860
		Telegraph line	Civil War	1861
			Homestead Act	1862
		Transcontinental railroad	Powell navigates Grand Canyon	1869
			Major Alaskan gold strike	1880

2

The Santa Fe Trail

EXPLORERS, TRAPPERS, AND TRADERS

The Santa Fe Trail is famous as the first American thoroughfare west of the Missouri River. But like all other trails over which the westward expansion was made, it was simply a route. Its course followed a multiplicity of age-old Indian trails westward along the Kansas, Smoky Hill, and Arkansas rivers. It is generally believed that Santa Fe was the first trading center in the Rockies, but this is a mistake. Taos Pueblo, seventy-five miles to the north, had been an important trading center for generations before the Spaniards arrived. There the Utes brought their Digger Indian slaves, and in coming to trade for them, the plains Indians wore deep trails between the Arkansas River and the Rio Grande. One of these ancient routes became the western section of the Santa Fe Trail.

Just as England taxed the Bostonians' tea, Spain taxed her colonists on all merchandise brought into her territories. She was extremely jealous of the trade and ruthless in her taxation. Goods from the United States were allowed to enter Mexico only through the port of Veracruz, and to reach Santa Fe this merchandise had to be transported two thousand miles on pack mules. The cost of transportation, the tax, and the Spanish merchants' unreasonable profits, resulted in fantastic selling prices. For instance, calico costing a few cents a yard in Boston, sold in Santa Fe for anywhere from two to three dollars a yard.

Zebulon Pike was the first American to bring back word of the exorbitant Santa Fe prices. In 1806 the United States Government sent him to explore the Louisiana Purchase, the western boundary of which was clearly stated to be the Continental Divide, but the southern boundary was indefinite, and Spain claimed it to be the Arkansas River. Pike followed the Arkansas into the foothills of the Rockies, then turned southward to the headwaters of the Rio Grande, where the Spanish arrested him as a spy invading their territory. They held him prisoner for a few days at Santa Fe, then sent him to Chihuahua for trial. Pike was not ill-treated, but following his exploration Americans were looked upon with suspicion by the Spanish Government.

It was 1807 before Pike was released, and probably several years later before the news he had brought trickled westward from Washington to Missouri. At the frontier town of Franklin, the most westerly American settlement, Robert McKnight and his brothers had a trading post where they carried on a thriving business with the Indians. When Robert heard of the fabulous prices goods were bringing in Santa Fe, he decided to go there with a merchandise caravan, and convinced James Baird and William Chambers to join him in the venture. They set out in April, 1812, with seven men and a small train of pack mules. Since they were using Pike's report as a guide, it is probable that they traveled along the Arkansas nearly to the present site of Pueblo, Colorado, then followed the age-old Indian trail up Huerfano Creek to the summit of the Sangre de Cristo range, and down the Rio Grande to Taos and Santa Fe. Upon reaching Santa Fe they were arrested, their stock of merchandise and mules confiscated, and they were sent to prison at Chihuahua, where they were held until Mexico won its independence in 1821.

By the time McKnight set out on his disastrous trad-

ing trip Pike's report of the great buffalo herds on the
Kansas prairies had spurred parties of frontier hunts-
men to push westward. One of these was led by Joseph
Philibert. In the spring of 1814 he left St. Louis with
eight or ten mounted hunters leading pack horses. They
rode up the Missouri to its northward turn, then followed old trails leading more directly to the great bend
of the Arkansas than those along the Kansas and
Smoky Hill rivers. Hunting westward along the Arkansas, they reached the foothills of the Rockies in late fall,
their supplies running low, and their pack horses loaded
with buffalo robes. In order to make an early hunt the
following spring, Philibert decided to leave most of his
men in camp at the mouth of Huerfano Creek while
he returned to St. Louis with the robes and brought
back supplies, together with bright colored cloth and
trinkets for trading with the Indians.

Philibert made his return journey without difficulty,
and disposed of his robes to the Chouteau Brothers fur-
trading firm. Auguste Pierre Chouteau, one of the
younger brothers, was much impressed by the size and
value of the robe packs, and proposer that he, Jules
DeMun, and Philibert join forces and organize a much
larger hunting and trapping expedition. The agreement
was made, and in the spring of 1815 the party marched
westward along the Arkansas. When they reached
Huerfano Creek they found the camp of the previous
fall deserted, and learned from nearby Indians that the
men had been forced by starvation to make their way
to Taos.

Knowing of McKnight's imprisonment, Philibert and
Chouteau were afraid to take their costly pack train
into Spanish territory. Instead, they sent De Mun with
an Indian guide to reach Taos and discover the fate of
the men. He found that they had passed the winter in
comfort, being fed and treated hospitality by the Pueblo
Indians and the few Mexicans living in the settlement.
For some unimaginable reason, De Mun decided to

continue on to Santa Fe and explain to the Spanish Governor the cause of their being in his territory. To his surprise, Governor Mainez received him with courtesy, and raised no objection to the American hunters having come into Spanish territory. Much relieved, De Mun gathered up the men at Taos and returned to his partners on the Arkansas, unwittingly setting the stage for American invasion of the Southwest.

Great buffalo herds covered the prairies that stretched northward from the Arkansas, but the creeks and rivers flowing into it from the Sangre de Cristo Mountains to the south were teeming with beaver, and Auguste Chouteau was wise in the ways of the fur business. Either a well-dressed buffalo robe or beaver pelt would bring six dollars on the St. Louis market, and one robe was as bulky to transport as a score of beaver pelts. The Philibert-Chouteau party began working its way up Huerfano Creek, trapping beaver as it went. The trapping was excellent. After reaching the summit of the Sangre de Cristos, the trappers sampled the headwaters of the Rio Grande enough to find that they were alive with beaver, then went on to Taos, where the men probably did a little bragging to their Mexican friends of the previous winter. After a hearty welcome they crossed the range again, and began trapping the headwaters of the Purgatoire River, dropping back to Taos whenever they found themselves running short of supplies.

By fall the beaver packs were bulging, and worth more than $30,000, but unfortunately affable Governor Mainez had been replaced by the American-hating Pedro Maria de Allande. On the trappers' next visit to Taos they were arrested, their fur packs, horses, traps and guns confiscated, and they were thrown in the *calabozo*. After forty days of being threatened by the Governor that they were to be shot as spies, they were turned loose, given a horse apiece, and told to get out. De Mun and Philibert returned to St. Louis, but

Chouteau remained in Kansas to become an important figure in the history of both the Santa Fe and Overland trails.

For six years following the Philibert-Chouteau confiscation American frontiersmen continued hunting along the western reaches of the Arkansas. Although they knew a fortune in beaver pelts to be in the mountain streams to the south, they kept to the north side of the river, and developed a trade more profitable than buffalo hunting. Mules were scarce and high priced in Missouri, but the Mexicans along the Rio Grande had plenty, and Indians were never averse to stealing. As soon as they discovered that American hunters would exchange trinkets and bright cloth for mules, they raided the Mexican herds mercilessly, drove the stolen animals to the north bank of the Arkansas, and traded them to whichever hunter would give them the most cloth and trinkets.

FATHER OF THE SANTA FE TRAIL

In the late summer of 1821, William Becknell put a notice in the *Missouri Intelligencer* that he was making up a party to go "westward for the purpose of trading for horses and mules and catching wild animals of every description." On September 1, his party crossed the Missouri and set out along the now well-traveled route to the Great Bend of the Arkansas, each leading a pack horse loaded with the sort of merchandise for which Indians liked to trade. It was late in the season for trading, the Indians had disposed of all their stolen stock, and were hunting in Spanish territory, so the Becknell party reached the present location of La Junta, Colorado, without having done any business. In desperation, Becknell turned southward and followed an age-old Indian trail up Timpas Creek, across Raton Pass, and down to the headwaters of the Canadian

River near present-day Maxwell, New Mexico. The next day the traders were surprised by a small troop of Mexican soldiers, and fully expected to be arrested. But the soldiers were delighted to see them, told them that Mexico had won its independence, that the Spanish Governor was gone, and urged them to take their goods to Santa Fe. Becknell reached the pueblo on November 16, opened a caravan trade that was to continue for more than forty years, and earned the title of "Father of the Santa Fe Trail."

Although the merchandise Becknell and his associates had brought was intended for trade with the Indians, it sold quickly at tremendous profit, and the payment was made in Spanish silver dollars. Most of the men decided to spend the winter in Santa Fe— and their easy profits on the Mexican *señoritas*. But Becknell and a man named McLaughlin loaded their saddle bags with silver and hurried back to Franklin, reaching that little frontier town on January 29, 1822. As an indication of the profit made, Fanny Marshall had lent her brother sixty dollars toward the amount necessary to buy his pack horse and trade goods; she received nine hundred dollars as her share of the profits.

News that Mexico was open to the Americans spread like a contagion along the frontier, and from far and near traders and trappers began gathering at Franklin. The trappers were for the most part the rough, tough soldiers of fortune who, as the mountain men, were to push the American frontier westward to the Pacific. The traders were men who had made their living by trading with the Indians along the Mississippi and Missouri, none of them having more than a few horses, a few packs of cheap merchandise, and a few dollars. Although Becknell's percentage of profit on his 1821 venture had been great, only a small amount of the goods had been his, so he was unable to finance as large a caravan as he wanted to take to Santa Fe in 1822. Consequently, he joined forces with other small merchants who were anxious to get into the Santa Fe trade.

Becknell's caravan, numbering twenty-one men, left Arrow Rock, across the Missouri from Franklin, on May 22. There is no record of the value of the caravan's cargo, how many pack horses there may have been, or how many of the men were financially interested in the venture. But it was the most important caravan ever to move over the Santa Fe Trail, for Becknell and two of his associates took their merchandise on wagons, the first to roll westward from the Missouri. It is quite likely that all the men not financially interested were trappers, for it is known that Ewing Young was among them.

Except for spring mud along the Missouri, the Becknell party had no trouble until it reached eastern Kansas, and the men were allowed to string out when a halt was necessary for pulling a wagon out of a mud hole. Not long after leaving the river, two of the men were riding far out in front when they were surprised by a small band of Osage Indians. They were severely beaten, robbed of their horses, guns, and clothing, and carried off to the Indian village. But, fortunately, Auguste Chouteau had established a trading post among the Osages, and was present when the captives were brought into the village. He at once secured their release, had their property given back, and accompanied them to the caravan. The incident was slight, but had great influence upon the manner in which caravans were conducted on the trail. Thereafter, a captain was appointed for each party, no spreading out was permitted, and guards were posted during the nights.

Mud, thickets, and flooded creeks were troublesome to the Becknell party in Missouri and eastern Kansas. Farther west the country became treeless prairie, somewhat hilly at first, then rising gradually and flattening out into great plains of short grass. There was abundant grazing for the animals, and wagon wheels rolled as easily as upon a roadway, the only difficulty being the necessity of cutting down a few steep creek banks.

Becknell followed the usual route through central Kansas to the great bend of the Arkansas, then continued southwest along the river to a point about five miles beyond where Dodge City now stands. It is known that he had hunted and traded with Indians in the area for several years, and he may have learned from them of the Cimarron River, farther to the south. The Cimarron rises just below the Colorado-New Mexico boundary, and flows eastward through the panhandle of Oklahoma nearly to the corner of Kansas. There it turns to the northeast and, like the Arkansas, forms a great bend, the apex of which is fifty miles to the southwest of Dodge City.

Whether or not Becknell had knowledge of the Cimarron, he did know that it would be almost impossible to get his wagons over Raton Pass, and that he could save about a hundred miles of travel if he could discover a direct route across the deserts to Santa Fe. Choosing a place where the Arkansas was more than a quarter mile wide but only three or four feet deep, he made his crossing and struck off to the southwest, with no landmarks and only a pocket compass by which to set his course. The only water carried was in the men's canteens, heat waves shimmered above the scorched land, and in sandy places the wagon wheels cut deeply, slowing progress and wearing down the mules. Becknell sent scouts far out ahead and to either side, but no sign of water was found, and in all directions flat semibarren land stretched away to the horizon. Before evening of the first day the canteens were empty and the wagon mules beginning to give out from heat and hard pulling.

Becknell went on through the night, setting his course by the north star and keeping the men afoot to

save the horses and mules as much as possible. By noon
of the second day the caravan was barely crawling, with
horses, mules, and men nearing the point of complete
exhaustion from heat and thirst. As the afternoon
dragged on one animal after another fell and was unable to rise. The men bled them, drank the blood, and
staggered on. When they had nearly lost hope and two
or three men had fallen out, a lone buffalo was seen
coming from the east. As he approached the men went
wild with excitement; his belly was distended with water,
and there was mud, not yet entirely dry, on his legs. He
was shot, slimy water from his paunch drunk greedily
by the men still able to keep their feet, and a canteen
of it taken back to those who had fallen.

Becknell had set his course amazingly well, for when
the buffalo's track was followed back it led, within a
few miles, to the bend of the Cimarron. With water
reached, the worst of the hardship was past, for the
river led in an almost straight line toward Santa Fe for
a distance of ninety miles. Although it, like many desert
streams, was often dry in summer, water could usually
be found by digging into the sandy bed. Between the
headwaters of the Cimarron and the Canadian rivers
lay another sixty-mile stretch of arid desert, but crossed
by a few creek beds in which water could be found by
digging. Becknell turned southward beyond the Canadian, picked up his trail of the previous year, and
followed it around the southern end of the Sange de
Cristo Mountains to Santa Fe, having traveled 870
miles since leaving Franklin.

Sources vary widely as to the value of merchandise
carried by the Becknell caravan of 1822, but it was
sold at an enormous profit, and Becknell returned to
Franklin by the route he had blazed, which was thereafter known as the Cimarron Cutoff.

Another party to set out for the Santa Fe trade in
1822 left its mark on the trail. When, after nine years'
imprisonment, Robert McKnight and his men were

released, McKnight remained in New Mexico, and for some years operated the copper mines near the headwaters of the Gila River. But James Baird and William Chambers returned to St. Louis. Baird was successful in persuading some merchants to finance them in a trading venture, but it was fall before they had gathered their stock of goods and pack animals at Franklin. Prudent men would have waited until spring, but Baird and Chambers were greedy for the huge profit that could be made if they reached Santa Fe by Christmas, so set out at once.

They had reached the point where Becknell had crossed the Arkansas when they were caught in a raging blizzard. Unable to travel, they made camp on a small island in the river, where they could best protect themselves from Indian attacks, but their pack animals wandered away and died. Being rugged frontiersmen, Baird and Chambers managed to keep alive until spring. As soon as the ground thawed, they dug deep holes on the island, lined them with grass, cached their merchandise packs, tramped the dirt firmly over them, and built fires so that ashes would hide signs of their digging from the Indians. Making their way afoot to Taos, they secured pack mules, returned, dug up their packs, and went on to Santa Fe. For more than twenty years the holes remained visible from the bank of the river, marked the crossing place for the Cimarron Cutoff, and was known as The Caches.

Except for Baird and Chambers, there is record of only one caravan reaching Santa Fe in 1823. This was a cooperative venture led by Stephen Cooper and is of importance for two reasons. When he returned to Franklin in October he not only brought the first fur packs shipped over the Santa Fe Trail, but four hundreds mules, jennies, and the Spanish jacks that sired the first Missouri mules.

CARAVANS AND COMANCHES

Along the Santa Fe Trail, as elsewhere throughout the West, the Indians were friendly until the white men taught them to be otherwise. The early hunters in southwestern Kansas encouraged the Indians to steal horses and mules from the Spaniards, and to trade a whole herd for a ten-dollar pack of trinkets and bright calico. The Indians soon learned that it was easier to waylay a small party and take the packs than to make the long journey into New Mexico and steal mules to trade for them. The beaver trappers who went over the Santa Fe Trail with the earliest traders were tough, ruthless frontiersmen, many of whom believed the only good Indian to be a dead one. On their way to the mountains they made many a good Indian, and made the Cheyennes, Comanches, and Kiowas the dreaded enemies of the traders.

By 1824 Auguste Chouteau had, through understanding and honest dealing, won the confidence and control of the Osage Indians along the Missouri Valley section of the trail, but on the prairies of Kansas and the deserts of New Mexico no small party was safe from attack. As a result, it became necessary for small merchants wishing to enter the Santa Fe trade to join together in large well-armed caravans.

On April 1, 1824, a meeting was held in Franklin for the purpose of organizing a Santa Fe caravan. It was not to be a cooperative venture. Each trader was to supply his own merchandise, pack animals or vehicles, and a guard for each eight animals or two wagons. The rendezvous was to be on May 5, and each man was to come equipped with a good rifle, a pistol, four pounds of powder, eight pounds of lead, and twenty days' provisions. Althought the journey was expected to require ten to twelve weeks, buffalo meat would furnish most of the rations as soon as the plains were reached.

It was May 16 before the caravan set out, consisting

of eighty-one men, one hundred and fifty-six horses and mules, twenty-five vehicles, and a small wheeled cannon for frightening away the Indians. Among the traders were M. M. Marmaduke who later became the Governor of Missouri, and Augustus Storrs who was appointed consul to Santa Fe in 1825. It is estimated that the total investment in mechandise was thirty-five thousand dollars. The caravan followed the Cimarron Cutoff route and reached Santa Fe on July 28. The merchandise, consisting mostly of cotton goods, a few woolens, small tools, needles, thread, buttons, trinkets, etc., was quickly sold at a profit of better than one hundred and fifty-five thousand dollars. With one hundred and eighty thousand dollars in silver and gold, and fur packs worth ten thousand dollars, the traders hurried back to Franklin in less than sixty days. Marmaduke and Storrs, both influential men in Missouri, rushed news of the fabulous profit to Senator Benton in Washington. It soon spread throughout the United States, making Missouri the most popular state on the frontier.

Thomas Hart Benton was the most rabid expansionist in the Senate. In the Santa Fe trade he saw not only an opportunity to push the boundaries of the United States westward, but an excellent opportunity to expand the population, commerce, and wealth of his own state. At Benton's request, Augustus Storrs prepared a statement of the "origin, present state, and future prospects of trade and intercourse between Missouri and the Internal Provinces of Mexico." The report would have done justice to a Madison Avenue copywriter. After delineating the course of the trail, Storrs noted that, "The face of the country, through which the route passes, is open, level, and free to the base of the Rocky Mountains . . . there is not a single hill of consequence, or which presents difficulties to the progress of a wagon." He wrote of the "high and perfectly level plain to the Semarone," but avoided mentioning the lack of water. After recommending that a road be surveyed at

Government expense, he suggested that peace treaties be negotiated with the nine Indian tribes through whose hunting grounds the trail passed.

Benton at once proposed a bill for building a road from the Missouri to the point of the Cimarron Cutoff on the Arkansas. From there to Santa Fe and Taos, with the approval of the Mexican Government, the best possible route was to be surveyed and markers set up. The bill passed both houses of Congress, and was signed by President Monroe two days before the expiration of his term. It carried an appropriation of thirty thousand dollars; ten thousand dollars for surveying and establishing the road, and twenty thousand dollars for buying rights of way from the Indians. Upon taking office, President Adams promptly appointed a Road Committee, including the Lieutenant Governors of Missouri and Illinois, and named Joseph Brown as surveyor.

When, on July 4, 1825, the surveying party set out from Franklin there was a great celebration—the most valuable part of the entire project. There was, of course, no actual intention of building a road. Brown's function was simply to discover, survey, and mark the most feasible wagon route to Taos and Santa Fe. He did his work as well as he could under the circumstances, finding the most practicable places for fording streams, describing the best possible line of travel from one ford to another, and marking the course with mounds of earth, since there were no stones on the prairies. Unfortunately, his detailed descriptions of the route were tucked away in some pigeonhole at Washington and lost for a generation, and within a year the wind had blown away the mounds of earth with which he had marked the trail.

The survey was barely started before the commissioners set out to pay twenty thousand dollars for the rights of way from the Indians. On August 10 they made a treaty with the chief of Auguste Chouteau's peaceful Osages at a beautiful grove, a hundred and forty miles southwest of present Kansas City. The commissioners promised the chief eight hundred dollars in merchandise for perpetual safe passage through his hunting grounds, and in honor of the occasion named the meeting place Council Grove. Fifty-five miles farther to the southwest they made a like treaty with the friendly Kansas Indians, then found a good excuse for turning back without visiting the dangerous prairie tribes: these people were nomadic, hunting over a vast area on both sides of the Arkansas, so it would be impossible to prove whether they were under the jurisdiction of the United States or Mexico, and it would be improper to make an American treaty with Mexican Indians. The only result of the commission's activity was the establishment of Council Grove as the great rendezvous point for caravans moving westward over the Santa Fe Trail.

The 1825 caravan was much like that of 1824, except that double the amount of merchandise was taken to Santa Fe, and the profit was far less than that of the previous year. The Mexican Government required an import tax equal to sixty percent of the cost of the goods to be paid before the merchandise could be sold. This drove out some of the smaller merchants, but those who continued in the trade increased the amount of goods taken, so as to maintain their profit level in spite of the tax. In 1824 eighty traders had carried goods which cost no more than thirty-five thousand dollars. In 1826 seventy traders carried goods costing ninety thousand dollars. In 1827 the number dropped to fifty with an equal amount of merchandise.

At the time Becknell set out on his first trading trip to Santa Fe, Franklin was the most westerly town on the American frontier, but as the trade increased towns sprang up farther along the river, and in 1825 the first settlers arrived at Independence. During the next few years small caravans started out from various river ports early in May, traveled separately through the peaceful land of the Osage Indians, and met for rendez-vous at Council Grove.

There, for mutual protection against the fierce prairie tribes, a single annual caravan was organized, and a captain chosen by vote of all the men, whether independent traders or hired hands. The captain appointed a wagon boss, a pack train boss, a chief scout, lieutenants for the various divisions, and a wrangler for the loose stock that was always driven along for replacements. Rules were laid down, the position of each division of the caravan set, and each man assigned his hours for night guard duty. Westward from Council Grove, the caravans usually traveled in three or four parallel columns, since there was no roadway and compactness made them more easily defensible. At night the wagons, carts, and carriages were formed in a square, pack animals unloaded and the packs stacked up to form a breastwork in case of Indian attack. In the late afternoon and early evening the stock was grazed as far out as a mile from the camp, but as darkness fell it was brought in, corralled inside the square for the night, or picketed close at hand to avoid possibility of a stampede by the Indians.

When Santa Fe was reached the caravans split up, some traders selling their merchandise from their wagons or packs, some renting little adobe buildings where they could set up shop, and some operating from corrals. For a few years following the imposition of the import tax the shrewder merchants preferred to trade their goods for horses and mules, since an animal costing fifteen or twenty dollars in Santa Fe would bring upwards of a hundred in Missouri. Because of this method of operation, all the traders were seldom ready to return at the same time. For this reason the caravans usually returned to Missouri in two or more divisions, fur packs and Mexican silver being carried in the otherwise empty wagons, and the herd driven along behind.

In August, 1828, the advance division started home-ward across the New Mexico deserts, some fifty or sixty men driving a herd of a thousand horses and mules behind a dozen or so wagons. The heat was almost intolerable, there was no breeze, and the dust rising from four thousand shuffling hoofs was so thick that a man could scarcely see a hundred feet ahead. As the party reached what is now the western end of the Oklahoma Panhandle, Daniel Munroe and a young man named McNees rode far ahead to find water. They found it in a little nameless creek, drank heartily, lay down on the bank, and went to sleep. When the caravan came up, McNees was dead and Munroe dying. Tracks showed that a small band of Indians had sur-prised them in their sleep, and shot them with their own guns. In panic, the traders scooped out a shallow grave in the sand, buried McNees, loaded Munroe onto one of the wagons, and pushed on as rapidly as the strag-gling herd could be driven.

By the time the Cimarron was reached, Munroe had died, and a stop was made for burying his body. It had barely been covered when six or seven Comanches rode into sight on the far side of the river. These certainly were not the Indians who had killed Munroe and McNees, or they would not have approached a force of fifty or more heavily armed white men without ap-parent fear. But the white men were both panicked and angry. As soon as the Indians came within range they were met with a fusillade of gunfire. Only one of them escaped to take word of the massacre back to their camp. Soon shrieking Comanches raced their ponies into the valley from all directions. The band was not large enough to give battle to so strong a force of white men, but in true Comanche fashion it circled the caravan, shrieking, yelling, and waving blankets until it had stampeded and driven away almost the entire herd of a thousand horses and mules.

Two weeks later the second division reached the

Cimarron, made up mostly of traders who had sold their goods for silver. Somewhat more than fifty thousand Mexican silver dollars were being transported in four or five wagons, behind which twenty-five men drove a herd of a hundred and fifty choice Mexican mules and horses. The Comanches had evidently been watching the progress of the party across the deserts, and had set an ambush for it at the location of the massacre. Although far outnumbered by the Indians, the little caravan was able to break out of the ambush, though the captain was killed and scalped.

The Comanches, like most other plains Indians, had no taste for open battle with well-armed white men, but they were superb horsemen, and harried their less skillful white enemies as wolf packs harried the buffalo herds. Across the Oklahoma Panhandle the Indians kept up a continual harassment, staying just out of gunshot in daylight, then sneaking in at night to stampede and drive away stock. By the time the corner of Kansas was reached, every horse and mule had been driven away. During daylight the traders stood off the Comanches by forting up in the wagons, but they were cut off from water and there was no possibility of holding out. When darkness fell they sneaked away to the north, each man carrying a little food and about a thousand silver dollars.

The Comanches evidently believed that it was only necessary to keep the white men from reaching water at the Cimarron, and that if they tried to escape to the north they would die of thirst before reaching the Arkansas. In any event, the men were not molested as they crept away. Staggering on without sleep or water for forty-eight hours, they made their way straight northward, reaching the Arkansas at Chouteau's Island, near the present Colorado-Kansas boundary. There was no possibility of carrying the silver any farther, so they cached it on the island and set out on the four-hundred-mile walk to Independence.

Until the bend of the Arkansas was passed the party had no great difficulty, for there was plenty of buffalo, no Indians were encountered, and the fall weather remained mild. Beyond the bend there were no buffalo, game became scarce, and the weather turned cold and stormy. Long before reaching the Missouri the men were nearing the point of starvation, and the less rugged became too weak to carry their firearms. East of Council Grove the five strongest went ahead to seek help, but found none until within fifteen miles of Independence. As rescuers hurried back along the trail they found exhausted men strung out for a distance of fifty miles, one of them blinded by starvation and fighting off wolves with a stick.

Several of the merchants who had suffered at the hands of the Comanches were influential men in Missouri, and when they returned, robbed and half-dead, immediate demands were made for military protection of travelers on the Santa Fe Trail. Benton delivered hours of oratory in the Senate, and when, on March 4, 1829, Andrew Jackson was inaugurated President, he directed that four companies of soldiers be assigned. The troops were to escort a caravan from the Missouri to the Mexican border beyond the bend of the Arkansas each spring, wait for it there, and escort it back in the fall.

There were two great faults in the plan. First, the Comanche attacks had taken place in territory claimed by Mexico, and it well might be considered an act of aggression if American troops crossed the Arkansas without permission from the Mexican Government. Secondly, the troops assigned were infantry, since there was yet no cavalry in the United States Army, and foot soldiers would have little chance in battle against mounted Indian warriors.

Most of the Missouri merchants decided that, considering the import tax, the inadequacy of military protection, and the growing hostility of the Indians, the risks of the Santa Fe trade were greater than any possibility of large profits. In 1829 the number of traders who joined the spring caravan dropped from eighty to twenty, but among them were the Bent brothers, whose names would be linked inseparably with the history of the Santa Fe Trail.

The first American beaver trapping expeditions went into the Rocky Mountains the year after Becknell's opening of the Santa Fe trade. That year General Ashley sent his famous party including Jedediah Smith, Tom Fitzpatrick, and Jim Bridger into the northern Rockies. Among the early trapper captains going over the Santa Fe Trail, all of whom made Taos their headquarters, were Ewing Young, Joe Walker, Old Bill Williams, and Ceran St. Vrain—son of one of the leading French fur-trading families of St. Louis.

THE BENT BROTHERS

For several years before the Ashley expedition, the Missouri Fur Company had been trading for pelts with the Indians, far up the Missouri. Among its members was twenty-one-year-old Charles Bent, the highly intelligent son of a St. Louis judge, a fearless pioneer, and contented only in the wilds of the frontier. He was small, black-haired, and though a descendant of the Massachusetts Pilgrims, so dark skinned that he was usually mistaken for a French Canadian, whose language, together with several Indian dialects, he spoke fluently. The trappers' coming to the mountains seriously curtailed fur trade with the Indians, and shortly before Ashley sold out to Smith, Sublette, and Jackson the Missouri Fur Company failed. Charles Bent and Joshua Pilcher then organized their own trapping party, and Charles was joined by his teen-aged brother William, also a natural frontiersman with amazing ability to learn the languages and win the confidence of Indians.

In the severe winter of 1827-28 the Pilcher-Bent party lost all its horses in a blizzard, was obliged to cache its packs, and encamped on the Green River in western Wyoming. In the same camp there was a party led by Ceran St. Vrain, which had also lost its horses in the blizzard. It is quite probable that during the winter encampment Charles Bent and St. Vrain laid plans to quit trapping and go into the Santa Fe trade. In any case, St. Vrain returned to Taos in the fall of winter encampment Charles Bent and St. Vrain laid pla 1828, and the Bent brothers to St. Louis. There the brothers disposed of their furs, bought trade goods, wagons and mules, and arrived at Independence on or about William Bent's twentieth birthday to join the 1829 Santa Fe caravan.

One by one the other eighteen traders arrived until, at the end of May, thirty-eight wagons, loaded with merchandise costing sixty thousand dollars, surrounded the few log cabins and warehouses of Independence. In all, there were seventy-nine men, including several who had survived the tragedy of the previous fall and cached their silver on Chouteau's Island. At the election Charles Bent, a natural leader, was unanimously chosen captain of the caravan.

The wagon had been ready to roll for more than a week before the promised escort of two hundred soldiers arrived from Fort Leavenworth. It was led by Major Riley, and second in command was Philip St. George Cooke, then only a second lieutenant two years out of West Point. The delay had been caused by Major Riley's mistake of crossing the Missouri and getting his little army mired in the bogs along the eastern bank. The traders were thoroughly disgusted, and several threatened to abandon the caravan, for the escort appeared to be more of a hindrance than a protection: not only were the infantrymen the riffraff of the frontier, commanded by an officer who knew no better than to lead them into swamps, but their sup-

ply wagons were being drawn by slow moving oxen.
The next morning, however, the caravan rolled out
onto the long trail. In the lead rode Major Riley, followed by the infantry, the ox-drawn supply wagons,
the mule-drawn traders' wagons, and a wrangler driving
the loose stock.

Presumably some of the disgruntled traders had
made it evident to Riley that they considered his escort
a hindrance rather than a protection. Otherwise, there
can be little excuse for his conduct. From the outset
it became apparent that the slow-footed oxen would
have no difficulty in keeping ahead of the fast-stepping
mules, for the mules had to be rested after each hard
pull, while the oxen continued to plod on. No doubt
in an attempt to strike back, Riley pulled away from
the traders' wagons enough that by the time Council
Grove was reached the night camps of the soldiers and
merchants were several miles apart. Charles Bent
protested, but since he had no authority over the escort,
he could only push the traders' division of the caravan along as rapidly as possible.

All went well through the hunting grounds of the
friendly Osages, and for a short distance beyond Council Grove. Then one morning, from long experience
gained in the mountains, Charles Bent recognized the
first sign of hostile Indians. He galloped his horse to
the soldiers' camp to warn the less experienced Riley,
but the warning was too late. During the night Indians
had stampeded the few horses brought along as officers'
mounts, and driven six of them away. The major had
scattered his infantrymen far and wide to run down the
thieves, but not so much as a hoof mark had been
found. The experience was well worth the few horses,
for Bent had little trouble in convincing Riley that all
the wagons should roll in a compact column, and that
the place for infantrymen was at the front and rear of
the column.

In addition, Charles Bent learned a lesson that would set the pattern for a great deal of the future travel throughout the West: oxen could not only out-travel mules in rough country, but also were evidently safe from Indian raids. Since no attempt had been made to steal Riley's oxen, Bent reasoned that plains Indians preferred buffalo meat, and would be tempted to steal only such animals as could be stampeded and driven away at high speed. He determined to try oxen in the Santa Fe trade. Before many years had passed they out-numbered mules better than four to one, and continued to do so throughout the early settlement of the West.

With the caravan united, no further Indian trouble was encountered along the Arkansas. At The Caches, Charles Bent prepared for the crossing, while Major Riley chose a camp site for awaiting the fall return. But the traders who had originally railed loudest against the escort lost their courage, and demanded that it remain with the caravan across the Cimarron Desert. When Riley refused, stating that he had no authority to enter Mexican territory, they insisted on continuing along the north bank of the Arkansas to Chouteau's Island. Bent was unable to dissuade them by pointing out that such a course would lengthen the journey by at least two days, and that if the Comanches intended an attack the place of crossing would make no differ-ence.

On July 10, Chouteau's Island was reached, the owners retrieved the thirty-odd thousand silver dollars cached there the preceding fall, and again the timid refused to cross into Mexican territory without the escort. Again Riley refused, but agreed to let the caravan take along a small cannon. With it to give the frightened traders a spark of courage, Bent persuaded them to continue.

The route Becknell had pioneered across the flat plain between the Arkansas and Cimarron was bad enough, but the crossing from Chouteau's Island was infinitely worse. The river flowed through shifting channels, over hidden potholes and beds of quicksand, and the land stretched away to the southward in a series of rolling sand hills and gullies. A full day of back-breaking labor was required to get the thirty-eight wagons across. Next morning the start was made for the Cimarron; every barrel, keg, and canteen filled with water. By late afternoon only nine miles had been traveled, and the caravan was toiling through a circular basin, toward a narrow gulch at its south end. In this dangerous situation Charles Bent kept the wagons as closely together as possible and sent three men to scout the gulch ahead, one beyond the east rim of the basin, and his brother William to the west.

William Bent was riding a mule that had been bought at Independence. Its slit ears showed it to have once been in the hands of the Comanches, and no mule passed through their hands without learning to hate them. With nothing but rolling sand hills visible in any direction, the plodding mule suddenly raised his head, swung his muzzle toward the west, and snorted. He could not have told young Bent a clearer story. There were Comanches to the west, and since there was no breeze to bring their scent from that direction they were close at hand.

Shouting and firing his rifle as a warning to the caravan, William set spurs to his mule barely before the Comanche war shriek rose from a gully less than a hundred yards to his right. Within moments scores of racing ponies boiled into sight, naked warriors lying flat against their necks, howling and letting fly a storm of arrows.

In the basin Jacob Coates and Bill Waldo, both veteran frontiersmen, raced their horses up the rim toward the sound. As they came over the edge the Indians swerved aside momentarily, unable to believe that any but a strong party would charge out to meet them. Instantly another wildly yelling band swept into the far end of the gulch. Instead of holding their ground, the men who had been sent to scout ahead whirled and raced for the wagons. The two on fast horses escaped, but Samuel Lamme, on a stiff-legged mule, fell behind and was riddled with arrows. His body had hardly hit the ground before half a dozen warriors were on top of it, stripping away his scalp. Then the two bands joined and raced shrieking toward the caravan.

Almost without exception, the traders panicked, but the Bent brothers knew the Indian aversion for charging into rifle fire. Shouting for the teamsters to pull their wagons into a circle, Charles and William leaped to the ground and ran toward the oncoming Indians, yelling the mountain men's battle cry. They were followed by eight or ten frontiersmen guards, firing and reloading as they ran. The show of fight was enough to turn the attack. The Comanches swung wide and circled the basin, howling like wolves in an attempt to stampede the mules, taunting, and waving Lamme's bloody scalp. While William and the few who had courage enough to join him held the Indians off, Charles managed to get the wagons pulled into a tight circle, with the draft mules and loose stock inside.

When trenches had been dug and breastworks thrown up, William and the frontiersmen backed toward the crude fortification, and the Comanches closed their circle tighter, slowing their ponies to the tireless lope of a prairie mustang. The pattern was a familiar one to men who had fought the Indians of the plains. The Commanches knew the range of muzzle-loading rifles, were circling just beyond it, and would keep up their siege until their ring was broken or thirst had won the battle for them.

Although the Indians of the Great Plains had relatively few firearms by 1829, they and their ponies were sufficiently familiar with rifle fire that, except at close range, they had little fear of it. But cannon fire was entirely unknown to them, and all Indians were inclined to ascribe anything unknown to the supernatural. Aware of this, Charles Bent had the little cannon pointed toward the back trail, loaded it heavily with powder and small shot that would scatter, and called for volunteers to ride for help from the troops. Waiting until deep twilight, he mounted the volunteers on the fastest horses in camp, then touched a spark to the cannon fuse. At the roar a gaping hole was ripped in the Indian circle. Frightened ponies stampeded, bucking and throwing their equally panicked riders, who scrambled to their feet and ran from the roaring demon they could not understand. Before the panic was over and the Comanches had returned to continue their siege from a safer distance the volunteers were well on their way to the Arkansas.

By daylight the troops arrived and the Comanches broke their widened circle, but continued their harassment from a greater distance, small parties racing in now and again in an attempt to stampede and scatter the stock. Again the caravan crept southward across the arid desert, with the Comanches following well beyond range of the white men's demon. The water barrels ran dry, the infantrymen staggered as they slogged through the sand, and thirst-crazed horses, mules, and oxen died by the score. At the end of the second day a sinkhole of stagnant water was found, so alkaline from evaporation that putrid minnows floated on the surface.

Riley called a halt and refused to take his troops farther into Mexican territory, and again the timid among the traders balked at going on without an escort, but had little choice. In trying to return to the Arkansas they would almost certainly lose the rest of their animals, then be marooned until the caravan came back in the fall. The upshot was that all the traders went on, while Riley returned to his camp on Chouteau's Island.

The troops had barely turned back before a hundred frightened Mexicans came whipping their jaded burros into the traders' camp. They had been out killing buffalo and drying the meat when attacked by the Comanches who were harassing the caravan. Although the Mexicans were out of ammunition and of no help in holding off the Indians, they knew where water could be found, and a few of the most daring agreed to make a break for Taos.

Day after day the beleaguered caravan crept on, across the wilderness to the Cimarron, through the Oklahoma Panhandle, and out onto the New Mexico deserts. By day the terrified Mexicans flocked around the wagons like sheep and at night crawled beneath them, while the few frontiersmen in the party held the Comanches at bay with rifle fire and an occasional blast from the little cannon.

Meanwhile one of the Mexicans reached Taos with news of the caravan's predicament. St. Vrain and Ewing Young gathered forty trappers, nineteen-year-old Kit Carson among them, and set of immediately across the Sangre de Cristo Mountains and out onto the desert. But the Comanches, gathering strength as the siege continued, now numbered several hundred warriors, and had no intention of letting their rich prize escape. Fighting like demons, they drove the trappers back toward the Sangre de Cristos, while young Carson raced to Taos for reinforcements. Fifty-five men turned out, bringing the number of mountain men to nearly a hundred, a force too formidable for any tribe of bow-and-arrow Indians to withstand. After a short, disastrous skirmish the Comanches retreated, to head back for the Arkansas and harass the less formidable infantrymen.

Out of the rescue of the 1829 caravan grew friendships which were to have an immense effect upon the westward expansion of the United States. Before Santa Fe was reached Charles Bent and Ceran St. Vrain had formed a partnership which would dominate the commerce between the United States and Mexico, make them the most influential men in New Mexico, and lead to its eventual conquest without the firing of a shot. An equally strong friendship developed between William Bent and Kit Carson, neither yet of age, but destined to have a greater influence than any other two men upon the success of the Santa Fe Trail, the subduing of the plains Indians, and the opening of the West.

Following the rescue in the deserts, the caravan turned aside from the route of previous years. To have the protection of the mountain men it crossed the Sangre de Cristo Range to Taos, opening the first wagon road in the Rocky Mountains, a route which became the Taos branch of the Santa Fe Trail.

At Taos the friends separated, St. Vrain remaining, and Charles Bent going on to Santa Fe with the other traders, over the old Spanish road along the Rio Grande. At the same time Young set off on a beaver-trapping expedition to the Gila River, taking Carson with him as camp boy. William Bent may or may not have gone to Santa Fe with Charles. If so, he soon returned to Taos, for that fall he joined a party of beaver trappers setting out for the headwaters of the Arkansas.

Since the merchandise brought to Santa Fe by the beleaguered caravan of 1829 was less than half the amount brought the previous year, it found a ready market at exorbitant prices, and the profits made by the traders were extraordinary. Furthermore, Charles Bent made a close friend of the *jefe politico* at Santa Fe, and through him secured a force of two hundred Mexican troops to escort the returning wagons back to the Arkansas. The return was made by way of Taos, where St. Vrain and some thirty mountain men joined the caravan to take their fur packs to the St. Louis market.

Again, on the waterless *jornada* between the Cimarron and Chouteau's Island, the caravan was attacked by a band of several hundred Indians, but this time

Arapahos instead of Comanches. The poorly armed
Mexican troops sallied out for battle, but the Indians
drove them back, killing the captain and a few soldiers.
At this point the mountain men joined the skirmish
and quickly turned it into a rout. They killed a score or
more of the attackers, and convinced Charles Bent
that mountain men were the only dependable escort
for caravans crossing the hunting grounds of plains
Indians. His conviction was strengthened when Chouteau's Island was reached. From the time of Riley's
return, his camp had been harassed by roving bands
of buffalo hunters from all the plains tribes, and at
best the infantrymen could only hold them at bay. Four
of Riley's men had been killed, numerous wounded, and
most of his stock had been killed or driven away. Bent
was obliged to lend him mules to get his camp equipment back to Fort Leavenworth.

Following Riley's sad experience the United States
Government decided to discontinue escorts on the
Santa Fe Trail until such time as mounted troops were
available. But in spite of the lack of escort and the
danger of Indian attack, sixty traders with seventy
wagons and merchandise costing one hundred and
twenty thousand dollars joined the 1830 caravan. Prom-
inent among them were Charles Bent and Ceran St.
Vrain, and at their insistence eighty rugged frontiersmen and mountain men were taken along as teamsters
and guards. This caravan pioneered a new route across
the Kansas plains, which thereafter became the mainline of the Cimarron Cutoff. It left the Arkansas seventeen miles beyond the point where Becknell had turned
off, and again joined his trail near present Satanta. This
route had numerous advantages. Although slightly longer than the Becknell route, there were a few landmarks
by which to set a course for the bend of the Cimarron,
there was less sand, and the waterless trek was reduced
by about a half day's journey. Although several Indian
attacks were attempted, each was turned into a rout

by the well-mounted frontier guards, and the caravan went through with little difficulty.

The success of the 1830 caravan led to 1831's seeing the greatest traffic on the Santa Fe Trail of the first two decades of its existence, as well as another of the many great tragedies of the early West. That year a quarter of a million dollars' worth of merchandise was freighted over the trail by three hundred and twenty men, more than seventy of them independent traders, and it is probable that oxen were used for the first time for this purpose. The flood of trade goods was so great that the Santa Fe market became glutted, prices dropped to less than half that paid the previous year, and many a trader went back to Missouri without having made his expenses. But the firm of Bent-St. Vrain prospered, sending its wagons down the old Spanish road along the Rio Grande, and as far into Mexico as Chihuahua.

How many separate caravans went over the Santa Fe Trail in 1831 is unknown, but two that left Missouri before that of Bent, St. Vrain & Company made history. In one was Josiah Gregg, who kept a diary and later wrote *Commerce of the Prairies,* an American classic describing the trail and caravan life in passing over it. In the second were four of the most famous mountain men—Jedediah Smith, William Sublette, David Jackson, and Tom Fitzpatrick.

Following the trappers' rendezvous of 1830 Smith, Sublette, and Jackson had sold out to the Rocky Mountain Fur Company, of which Fitzpatrick was a member, probably agreeing to bring supplies for the following season as far as Santa Fe. In any case, the partners entered the Santa Fe trade in 1831. Tom Fitzpatrick met them at Independence, and they set out with a caravan of twenty-three wagons, loaded with trappers' supplies and trade goods. They crossed the Arkansas River near present Fort Dodge, planning to follow Becknell's original Cimarron Cutoff route.

No four men in the world had pioneered more trails

through unknown mountains and wildernesses, but they became lost on the flat, arid plain where there were no landmarks. With their water supply gone, mules dying by the score, and men falling in their tracks, Jed Smith and Tom Fitzpatrick rode ahead to find the Cimarron. Fitzpatrick's horse soon gave out and Smith rode on alone. Months later an Indian told the story of his death. A band of shrieking Comanches had surrounded him and panicked his thirst-crazed horse. Before Smith could bring it under control the Indians swarmed in and lanced him to death, but not until he had killed their chief. His grieving companions made their way to Taos, where Fitzpatrick gathered a party of trappers, and headed back into the Rockies. Among the men was Carson, just returned from California with Ewing Young, and soon to become famous throughout the mountains as leader of the Carson Men.

The Brent, St. Vrain & Company caravan went through without trouble. Leaving his partner to dispose of the goods, Charles Bent set out with a few well-mounted frontiersmen for a fast trip back to Missouri. By August he was in St. Louis buying goods, and in early September left Independence with another large caravan, the first ever to be pulled over the Santa Fe Trail entirely by oxen. The year 1831 not only marked the beginning of ox-drawn caravans, but the withdrawal of the peddler merchants from the Santa Fe trade. Thereafter the commerce was largely on a wholesale basis, with the firm of Bent, St. Vrain & Company dominating the field.

BENT'S FORT AND THE RIVER PORTS

While Charles Bent and Ceran St. Vrain had been establishing themselves as the leading American merchants in northern Mexico, William had been off on a venture of his own. From the time he had first gone to the mountains as a teen-aged boy, his greatest interest had been in Indians, and in dealing with them. The beaver-trapping party he had joined in the fall of 1829 worked the streams flowing into the Arkansas from the Sangre de Cristo and Front ranges of the Rockies, and made its base camp at the present site of Pueblo, Colorado.

Probably in the spring of 1830, William Bent returned to the base camp of the year before, not to trap beaver, but to trade with the plains Indians for buffalo robes. Little is known of his early operations, except that he built a log trading post, his business prospered, and he made a lifelong friend of the Cheyenne chief, Yellow Wolf.

Legend has it that Yellow Wolf urged young Bent to move his trading post seventy-five miles down the Arkansas, to the vicinity of present-day La Junta, since trails of all the prairie tribes crossed there and he would have a larger trade. This may be so, but it is much more probable that William chose the location because it was in the heart of the buffalo hunting area, near the only available timber east of the foothills, and at the point where the old Indian trail that Becknell had originally followed left the Arkansas. There was, however, great danger in such a move, for the location was the traditional battleground of the fiercest prairie tribes—the Comanches, Kiowas, and Jicarilla Apaches from south of the Arkansas; the Cheyennes, Arapahos, and Pawnees from the north. A trading post could be successful there only if strongly fortified and garrisoned.

There has been considerable disagreement among historians as to when Bent's Fort was built, and who its owners were. Recent research makes it almost certain that the original venture was a partnership between the Bent brothers and St. Vrain, though William was the sole operator. The entire plan must have been worked out during the summer of 1832, and it is evident that the Bent brothers had been extremely successful before that time. In November of that year they arrived at Independence with a large drove of Mexican mules, a cargo of silver bullion, and fur packs and buffalo robes reported by the local newspaper to be worth one hundred and ninety thousand dollars. In the spring of 1833 William returned with a caravan of equipment and armament for the fort, and it is known to have been completed in 1834.

Bent's Fort was built on the north side of the Arkansas River, and flew the only American flag west of the Missouri. The main structure was 178 by 137 feet, with the solid adobe walls four feet thick and fourteen feet high, the upper portion loopholed for defenders' rifles. Projecting from diagonal corners were turrets, providing a clear view of the outer side of the walls, and enabling defenders to repulse any attempt to scale them. The only entrance was a square tunnel, large enough for a prairie schooner to pass through, and closed at each end by a ponderous plank door armored with heavy sheet-iron. On either side were windows where Indians could come to trade without being admitted to the main fort. Above the tunnel rose a square watchtower, where swivel cannons were mounted, powerful enough to command the river and surrounding prairies for a distance of a mile or more. At the center of the structure there was a great courtyard, with space for a caravan of wagons. Surrounding it were living quarters, kitchens, arsenal, workshops, storage rooms for a hundred tons of buffalo robes and fur packs, and warehouses capable of holding a two years' supply of provisions and trade goods.

William Bent, like Theodore Roosevelt, believed that the best way to avoid war was to "walk softly and carry a big stick." His fort, with seldom less than a hundred defenders, was the stoutest stick west of the Missouri, but he walked softly among the Indians, winning their confidence by honest dealing, marrying a chief's daughter, and continually widening his trade circle. By the

time the fort was completed his influence among the
plains tribes had become so great that there was never
danger of attack.

Becknell's original route had fallen into disuse, as it
was impossible to get wagons over it, but during the
building of the fort it was cleared and roughly graded
into a usable wagon road. Its opening and the establishment of the fort, split travel over the Santa Fe
Trail roughly in half. With the Kiowas and Comanches
almost constantly on the warpath, the Cimarron Cutoff
was safe only for large, heavily guarded caravans, and
the loss of animals was always great in crossing the arid
deserts. Although nearly a hundred miles longer, the
route by way of Bent's Fort was safer from Indian attack, and since it followed the Arkansas River, Timpas
Creek, and the foothills of the Sangre de Cristo Mountains all the way there was less loss of stock from thirst.
The result was that the great annual caravans continued
to cross the cutoff, but most of the other traffic went
by way of the fort.

The Bent brothers could not have chosen a better
time to quit trapping and turn their attention to the
Mexican and Indian trade of the Southwest. By 1834
the streams of the Rockies were rapidly being trapped
out, and within five years most of the trapper bands
had left the mountains, many of the men becoming
buffalo hunters on the prairies.

By 1833 buffalo hunting had become a thriving industry, the Mexican trade was booming, the Santa Fe
Trail worn into a deep-rutted road, and Bent's Fort
had become the frontier headquarters. There travelers
stopped to rest their teams before making the hard pull
over Raton Pass. White hunters brought rough-dried
hides to market, and Indian bands came from far and
near to pitch their wigwams outside the walls and trade
their velvet-soft buffalo robes for the white man's goods.
Whoever came—Indian, trader, hunter, or traveler on
the trail—he was William Bent's guest.

To feed his guests, together with his hundred or more regular employees, required at least a thousand pounds of buffalo meat a day. But buffalo were becoming scarce in the area, and meat could no longer be hunted from day to day. When the herds migrated in spring and fall a crew of hunters had to follow them to the north and south, killing hundreds, drying the meat, and packing it back to the fort on mules. Each year this hunting became more dangerous, particularly to the south of the Arkansas, for the Kiowas and Comanches considered the buffalo theirs. Although these southern tribes came peaceably to the fort to trade, their hatred for the whites increased as the buffalo herds thinned. Attacks on caravans crossing the Cimarron Cutoff became more vicious, and few bands of white hunters dared to invade Comanche or Kiowa territory.

When, in 1838, beaver trapping became unprofitable, Kit Carson brought his already famous Carson Men to Bent's Fort and contracted to keep it supplied with buffalo meat. Since hunting to the north of the Arkansas might incur ill feeling among the friendly Cheyennes and Arapahos, Carson set out with five of his men to scout for herds in the southeastern corner of Colorado, the center of the Comanche hunting grounds. They were attacked by a war party of two hundred warriors when on an arid plain with no cover from which to fight. Carson leaped from his mule, slashed its throat, and shouted for his men to come in close and do the same. The men had barely time to throw themselves prone behind their still kicking mules before the Indians charged, but their ponies panicked at the smell of fresh blood, swerved to either side and raced past. Three Carson Men fired, and three Comanches fell. In a frenzy of rage the Comanches fought their ponies into a tightly packed, trampling mass and charged again and again. The carcasses of the dead mules bristled with arrows, but at the last moment each charge split, and each time three Carson Men fired. With more than twenty of their number killed, the Comanches took up their death circle, just beyond rifle range and at a jogging trot.

Comanches were among the most superstitious Indians on the prairies. They would never go into battle without a medicine man, and if his incantations failed to bring victory it was considered a sure sign that his medicine had lost its power. He must either commit suicide or be shamed by the entire tribe and lead a dog's life.

With the Comanches in their death circle, the only hope for the hunters was that Carson could bluff the Indians into thinking his medicine stronger than that of their medicine man. One of his men, who had been captured by the Comanches as a boy, spoke their language perfectly. Carson had him shout insults at the medicine man, telling him his medicine was antelope milk as compared to Carson's. When darkness came, Kit would scatter his strong medicine on the night wind, and the weeping squaws would come in the morning to gather the Comanche dead.

The strategy worked, for the medicine man was in a desperately tight spot. Dancing, chanting, and waving charms, he worked himself and the warriors into a frenzy. Then, leaping on his pony, he raced ahead of them toward the barricade.

Holding his men back, Carson stepped out a few paces to meet the charge. As the Indians raced into rifle range he took careful aim at the medicine man's throat, waited for the ponies to get close enough to smell blood, squeezed the trigger, and dropped flat as a storm of arrows whizzed above him. At the instant the ponies panicked he leaped to his feet again, giving the Comanches the impression that their arrows had hit but not harmed him. They had no stomach for testing the strength of his medicine on the night wind, and streaked back toward the Cimarron.

The legend of Carson's strong medicine spread like prairie fire among the plains tribes, extended beyond himself to the Carson Men, and had great effect upon the safety of travel over the Santa Fe Trail. It was seldom that the leader of a war party would knowingly attack a caravan or party guarded by Carson Men, whether or not Kit was present. When not hunting buffalo for Bent's Fort, they were kept busy guarding traders on the Santa Fe Trail.

In 1839 a significant change in the Santa Fe trade occurred. Mexican Governors were always susceptible to bribes, but in 1839 Governor Armijo put matters on a more businesslike basis. He announced that he would allow no American goods to enter New Mexico unless he received a rakeoff of $500 on each wagon load, regardless of its size. This squeezed the small merchants out of the Santa Fe trade, and the large firms were forced to change their method of operations. Where most of the wagons had been no larger than could be pulled by four mules or oxen, it was now necessary that each vehicle carry the greatest possible load. To accomplish this, enormous prairie schooners were built and put into Santa Fe trade, some of them requiring as many as thirty oxen. The Armijo gouge was beneficial to the Bent brothers. It not only increased their caravan business, but the additional tax drove countless Mexicans into trading their hides and furs for American goods at Bent's Fort.

By 1842 Independence had become second only to St. Louis as a river port, for it was the starting point of both the Santa Fe and Oregon trails. Each spring greater numbers of emigrants were setting out for the Northwest, and each year the traffic over the Santa Fe Trail was expanding. At the height of the spring season the town was overrun with emigrants, river men, trappers, buffalo hunters, traders, and teamsters, fighting over the scant grazing for their thousands of horses, mules, and oxen.

The Bent brothers, with seldom less than five hundred head of livestock at Independence, decided they must have their own headquarters, far enough from town to keep their teamsters away from the saloons and gay houses, and to relieve the grazing shortage. They chose a location called Westport Landing—now Kansas City—where there was a natural rock levee and cargoes could be transferred directly between wagons and riverboats. Within a year Westport Landing, rather than Independence, had become the eastern terminus of the Santa Fe Trail.

For the next four years larger and larger caravans rolled over the Santa Fe Trail with little difficulty, and protected by the Carson Men. Charles Bent and Ceran St. Vrain became firmly established as the leading merchants in New Mexico, and William extended his influence throughout the Great Plains, making Bent's Fort the largest American trading center west of St. Louis.

THEN CAME THE SOLDIERS

At the outbreak of the Mexican War the Santa Fe Trail became the military road of the West, seeing its greatest concentration of traffic during the spring and summer of 1846. In May the annual spring caravan left the Missouri with four hundred and fourteen prairie schooners, about eight thousand draft animals, and more than five hundred men. At the same time Colonel Stephen Watts Kearny was at Fort Leavenworth recruiting his Army of the West. His instructions from the War Department were to march over the Santa Fe Trail, conquer New Mexico, establish a government there, and move on for the conquest of California, but to interfere as little as possible with the spring caravan.

Early in June, Kearny began sending supply trains ahead at intervals of three or four days, each made up of from twenty-five to thirty wagons. The main supply caravan, consisting of a hundred wagons, set out near the end of the mouth, and on June 30 Kearny left Fort Leavenworth with a baggage train of three hundred wagons, an artillery battalion, and 1750 mounted dragoons. The dragoons were Missouri volunteers, the flotsaw of the frontier, and described by Ruxton, the great historian of the early West, as, "the dirtiest, rowdiest crew I have ever seen collected together."

The Army of the West was scarcely under way before it became more or less disorganized. There was no roadway between Fort Leavenworth and Elm Grove, the point at which Kearny decided to intercept the Santa Fe Trail. The first day's march was made through pouring rain, then the weather turned hot and humid. Before Elm Grove was reached on July 4, the Army was strung out for twenty miles or more, sweating mules and horses wallowing in a sea of mud, while swearing dragoons tugged at ropes to help pull the wagons and artillery out of the mire.

When the hard-packed wheel ruts of the Santa Fe Trail were reached the Army of the West pushed forward, singing and shouting, more in joy that the mud had been passed than in celebration of Independence Day. For the rowdy, undisciplined volunteers, the expedition became more of a lark than a march to war. They were for the first time heading for "wild Injun and buffala country," and every dragoon's trigger finger became itchy as the column neared the bend of the Arkansas. There the first great herd of buffalo was seen, estimated to have been more than half a million, and the few Regular Army officers were unable to enforce discipline. Although hunters had been sent ahead to supply meat for the troops, the dragoons shot thousands of buffalo for sport, and left their carcasses to rot on the prairies. Indians who came within musket range were sniped at, and those at a distance were frightened away by cannon fire.

Roistering and enjoying themselves, the dragoons caught up with and passed the advance supply wagons, then the great caravan, and arrived at Bent's Fort during the last week of July. Camp was pitched eight miles east of the fort, and Kearny went forward to confer with the Bent brothers. It was their belief that, although Governor Armijo had recruited troops for defense, there would be no great resistance by the New Mexicans. They pointed out that the people of Santa Fe had little direct contact with the Mexican capital, had for the past decade looked to the United States for their trade, and considered the Americans their friends.

Kearny remained skeptical, and took no action until July 31. At that time James Magoffin arrived from Washington with secret orders from President Polk. He conferred with Kearny, and requested a detachment of ten dragoons to escort him to Santa Fe under a flag of truce. Shortly after the conference, the colonel sent for Captain Philip St. George Cooke, instructed him to accompany Magoffin to Santa Fe, and gave him a letter to be delivered to Governor Armijo. The letter stated that the United States was annexing all of New Mexico lying east of the Rio Grande, and warned the Governor against trying to resist the formidable Army of the West.

Possibly because of rumors that Armijo had been reinforced and planned an ambush in the vicinity of Raton Pass, Kearny did not send Cooke and Magoffin ahead, but started his march of invasion on August 2. The temperature rose to 112°, the summer had been dry in the Sangre de Cristo, and Timpas Creek, a brawling torrent in spring and fall, was reduced to a brackish trickle. Without knowing where he might meet Armijo and his forces, Kearny was unable to send his supply wagons ahead. The dragoons and their horses drank what little water there was, and the supply train fell far behind, thirst-crazed mules dying by the hundreds. Leaving the trail pockmarked with abandoned wagons and dead mules, the teamsters drove on as best they could, trying to keep the dragoons supplied. But before Raton Pass was reached the men were on one-third rations, and in the sweltering heat they were dying by the dozen from dysentery and exhaustion.

Magoffin and Cooke hurried ahead under a flag of truce, but the Army of the West could barely creep, Kearny hoping not to meet the enemy until the mountains had been crossed and what was left of his supply train brought up. The march to the Mora branch of the Canadian River required twelve days. Nothing had been heard from Magoffin or Cooke, but Kearny received a message from Governor Armijo, "If you take the country it will be because you are strongest in battle. I suggest to you to stop at the Sapillo, and I will march to the Vegas. We will meet and negotiate on the plains between them."

Since the message was ambiguous, the Army of the West marched on to Las Vegas, but there was no sign of a Mexican army, and no one had been sent to negotiate. Posting a strong guard, Colonel Kearny went to bed. At midnight he was awakened by officers who had just ridden in from Bent's Fort, bringing news of his promotion to the rank of lieutenant general. But while the general was being congratulated on his promotion, the glory of conquering New Mexico was being taken from him.

What James Magoffin's secret orders from President Polk may have been, how he carried them out, and whether or not he divulged any part of them to Kearny is unknown. From the resuts, however, certain conclusions have been drawn. California was of tremendous value and western New Mexico of practically none, but Kearny's orders were to take New Mexico first, then move on for the capture of California. It is more than probable that the President feared France or England might seize California if Kearney were long delayed in the conquest of New Mexico. Doubtlessly, Magoffin's secret orders were to undermine Armijo by disaffecting Mexican Army officers, using western New Mexico as a bribe if necessary. It is also probable that

Through all the years that Taos had been the headquarters of the American mountain men they had had
no trouble with the Pueblo Indians, for rough and tough
as they were, the trappers had respected the gentle
Pueblo men and left their women alone. But as soon as
dragoons were brought into New Mexico they attempted to molest the Indian women, and the Pueblos
grew bitter toward Americans. Taking advantage of
this hostility and the fact that Carson and his men were
in California with Frémont, Don Diego Archuleta led
a band of his native followers to Taos. They plied the
Indians with whiskey, and stirred them into a general
uprising against the Americans, planned for Christmas
Eve. The plot was discovered, and Archuleta escaped
to Chihuahua with his followers, but the Pueblo Indians
remained sullen and angry.

Charles Bent had made his home in Taos since the
time of his marriage, and continued it there after his
appointment as Governor, traveling as often as possible from Santa Fe to visit his family. He was in Taos
on January 18, 1847, when the Indians suddenly re-
volted, flocked from their pueblo into the little town,
and were joined by a rabble of Mexican peons.

Throughout the night the anger of the mob increased
as jugs of Taos lightning passed from hand to hand and
rabble-rousing Mexicans inflamed the Indians with
tirades against the Americanos. Charles Bent, his wife,
and Carson's wife who was living with them, had plenty
of chance to escape to Santa Fe, but Bent, who had
always been on the friendliest of terms with the Pueblo
Indians and Taos Mexicans, could not believe they
would do him or his family harm. When, on the morning of the 19th, an angry mob gathered in front of his
house, he went to the door to reason with them, but
mob hysteria had risen beyond the point of reason.
He was shot down, scalped while still alive, and his body
riddled with knife wounds. The women and children

escaped only because of the bravery and loyalty of the household servants.

Twenty other Americans were killed in the rebellion, and though the leaders were tried and executed the smoldering embers of hatred had been fanned into a blaze. The plains Indians had been angered by the dragoons on their way west. Rebellion spread throughout the entire region, and no caravan passed over the Santa Fe Trail without being attacked. Forty-seven Americans were killed, three hundred and thirty wagons looted and burned, and more than sixty-five hundred head of stock butchered or run off. From the time William Bent had first begun trading with the Indians, his influence had kept the Cheyennes and Arapahos at peace with the white men, but the rebellion soon spread to them, too. Trade was brought to a standstill, and for the first time Bent's Fort was attacked. Troops on the Santa Fe Trail were no safer than caravans. Lieutenant Love, commanding a company of dragoons and carrying three hundred thousand dollars to pay the troops at Santa Fe, was attacked, had five men killed, six wounded, and lost a large number of horses.

To keep the plains Indians under any reasonable control was to cost the United States more than forty million dollars during the next fifteen years, but the Santa Fe Trail had to be kept open for supplying not only the troops but the twenty thousand newly acquired American citizens of New Mexico. Forts were built along the route, and strong troops of cavalry patrolled the trail. Government supply wagons and merchants' caravans continued to roll, but with Charles Bent's death and the uprising of the Cheyennes and Arapahos the heyday of Bent, St. Vrain & Company drew rapidly to a close. In August, 1849, William stripped the fort of everything valuable, touched a match to the arsenal, and blew the great landmark of the western prairies into a heap of rubble. Although the California gold rush was reaching its climax, there was little trade to be had from it. Only about eight thousand Argonauts went west by way of the Santa Fe Trail, due to the danger of Indian attacks.

In 1850 monthly mail and passenger service was established between Independence and Santa Fe, and was glowingly announced in the *Missouri Commonwealth:* "The stages are gotten up in elegant style, and are each arranged to convey eight passengers. The bodies are beautifully painted and made water-tight, with a view of using them as boats in ferrying streams. The team consists of six mules to each coach. The mail is guarded by eight men, armed as follows: Each man has at his side, fastened in the stage, one Colt's revolving rifle, in a holster below, one of Colt's long revolvers, and in his belt a small Colt's revolver, besides a hunting knife, so that these eight men are ready, in case of attack, to discharge 136 shots without having to reload. This is equal to a small army armed as in ancient times, and from the look of the escort, ready as they were either for offensive or defensive warfare with the savages, we have no fear for the safety of the mails." Passengers felt less confidence for their own safety and were scarce for several years.

Although relatively few Forty-Niners went to California by way of the Santa Fe Trail, the gold rush sparked the great westward expansion, and in spite of Indian depredations traffic over the trail increased rapidly. By 1855 the Santa Fe trade alone amounted to five million dollars. In 1865 three thousand merchandise wagons rolled westward over the trail, in addition to a continual stream of Army traffic. In 1866 the number of merchandise wagons increased to more than five thousand. Towns and way stations lined the route far westward into Kansas. The great buffalo herds were gone from the prairies, streams had been bridged, and Concord coaches sped east and west night and day, carrying thousands of passengers and hundreds of tons of mail and express, but by the end of the year the Santa Fe Trail had passed its peak.

In 1863 the first steel rails had pushed westward from Wyandotte, Kansas, across the river from Kansas City. Hundred of Indian attacks, the progress was slow, but by 1866 the rails had been extended to Junction City, a hundred miles west of the Missouri, and to meet them the Santa Fe Trail veered northeastward from the great bend of the Arkansas. Year by year the rails crept toward the southwest, and the Santa Fe Trail terminated at each new railhead. By 1872 the rails had reached the point where, a half century before, Becknell had crossed the Arkansas to pioneer the Cimarron Cutoff. There Dodge City, the cowboy capital of the West, was laid out, shipping in its first year nearly a quarter million cattle driven north from Texas, an equal number of buffalo hides from the Great Plains, and countless tons of merchandise coming and going over the shortened Santa Fe Trail.

For a year the railhead terminus of the trail was at Kit Carson, Colorado. Then the Kansas Pacific extended a branch southward to the approximate site of old Bent's Fort, and the Cimarron Cutoff fell into disuse. For a few years freight wagons and stagecoaches rolled over the rugged stretch of road the Bent brothers had cleared while building their fort, following the age-old Indian trail that Becknell had traveled in 1821, up Timpas Creek and over Raton Pass. Then in 1879 Raton Tunnel was completed. On February 9, 1880, the first train rolled into Santa Fe, and the Santa Fe Trail withdrew into the annals of American history.

3

The Big Medicine Trail

THE FUR TRADE

Thomas Jefferson had been keenly interested in the fur-rich Northwest for more than twenty years before becoming President. His original interest was aroused by John Ledyard, a brilliant Connecticut boy who had sailed with the famous British explorer, Captain James Cook, in his futile search for the Northwest Passage.

In the spring of 1778, Cooke had rounded South America, rediscovered the Hawaiian Islands, and was sailing toward Alaska when his ship was caught in a severe storm. After being driven eastward for several days, he sighted land and found refuge in a harbor, later known as Nootka Sound, on the western side of Vancouver Island. He had no sooner entered the sound than his ship was surrounded by scores of great canoes, skillfully handled and loaded to the gunwales with happily shouting Indians. They were decked in a profusion of well-tanned furs—bear, wolf, fox, skunk, marten, mink, and sea otter—and many of them wore U-shaped pieces of iron or copper, looped through incisions in their noses and earlobes.

Cook was more amazed at finding metal among these Indians than at their great wealth in furs. He knew that no British ship had ever before been in these waters, and was unaware that the Russians had been so far south, or that a Spanish ship had anchored in Nootka

Sound three years earlier. Believing the nearest source of fabricated metal to be a trading post at Hudson's Bay, he reasoned that these Indians had either traveled that far east, or that the metal had been brought to the Pacific coast through trade between the intervening tribes.

As soon as the anchor had been dropped, the Indians swarmed aboard, overrunning the deck and trying to make off with any piece of loose metal they could lay hands upon. It soon became apparent that they valued nothing highly except metal, and would trade anything to get it—including young female slaves captured from other tribes. Captain Cook drew the line at slaves, but being bound for the Arctic where warm clothing and bedding would be needed, he let his men trade pieces of metal from the ship for a considerable number of sea-otter pelts.

When the storm abated. Cook claimed the entire region by right of original discovery for the British Crown, and sailed away to the north. Beyond Bering Strait, and at the gateway to the actual Northwest Passage, he was forced back by impassable ice floes, so he returned to the Hawaiian Islands, where he was killed in trying to recover a stolen landing cutter. Lieutenant James King then took command and turned back toward England by way of the Orient, stopping at Macao Roads in China for repairs. While there, he went up the river to Canton, taking along twenty rather poor sea-otter furs in hope of trading them for a few badly needed supplies. To his amazement, the Cantonese were enthralled by the soft, dark furs. The twenty pelts sold for eight hundred dollars, and the Cantonese begged King to bring more. The clamor was so great that an auction was arranged on shipboard, at which prime sea-otter pelts brought $120 each.

Following the auction, King's crew nearly mutinied in their demands that he return to Nootka Sound. When he refused, two of the sailors deserted, determined to find their way back and become wealthy from the sea-otter trade. John Ledyard realized the folly of the desertions, since trade by sea could be carried on only by men with sufficient capital to outfit and man a ship, but an idea began shaping itself in his mind. The Nootka Indians were primarily boatmen and, if their iron and copper had come from Hudson's Bay, there were probably rivers that could be navigated for most of the distance. There must, also, be streams flowing into Hudson's Bay from the southwest, their headwaters near those of the Connecticut River. If so, a man with very little capital could get into the sea-otter fur trade, transporting bales of pelts from the Pacific Northwest to markets on the Atlantic coast by canoe.

Sea-otter furs became an obsession to John Ledyard, and he determined to discover a water route by which he could transport them across the continent, but his enlistment in the British Navy still had three years to run, and he learned in China that the United States was at war with England. Following the war, he succeeded in selling Thomas Jefferson, then Minister to France, on the potential value of the sea-otter fur trade to the United States, and the advantages of a transcontinental trade route between the Atlantic coast and the North Pacific. He then proposed and secured Jefferson's backing for one of the most fantastic schemes in history: he would cross Russia and Siberia to Kamchatka, find a means of reaching Vancouver Island, and discover a transcontinental water route back to New England. Afoot and in winter, Ledyard crossed Russia; he had reached central Siberia when he was arrested and turned back by the suspicious Russians. Heartbroken, he died a few years later, but his foresight was to have a profound effect upon the future history of the United States.

While John Ledyard was plodding across Russia, British sea captains were racing one another around South America and toward Vancouver Island, each in-

tent upon reaching Canton with a cargo of sea-otter
pelts before the market was glutted and the price fell.
But Chinese demand for the soft, dark furs was insati-
able. Profits from the sea-otter trade became enormous,
and the Pacific Northwest the most coveted and con-
troversial region on earth. Spain claimed exclusive ownership as far north as the present site of Anchorage,
Alaska, by right of original discovery in 1775. Although
the Spanish claim of prior discovery was legitimate, the
British refused to recognize it, and completely dominated the Northwest fur trade, sailing their trading
vessels into every bay or inlet from Puget Sound to the
Gulf of Alaska.

To enforce its claim of sovereignty, Spain sent war-
ships to Nootka Sound, seized two British vessels as
prizes, and took them to Mexico, with their crews im-
prisoned below decks. But Spain had passed the heyday of her power. When threatened with retaliation by
the British Navy, she capitulated. In the Nootka Sound
Convention of 1790, she virtually abandoned her claim
to exclusive ownership of the Pacific Northwest by
granting British subjects the right to trade or settle
on lands not currently occupied by Spanish subjects.

Although the British controlled the Northwest fur
trade, a few Yankees had taken a small part in it.
Among them was Captain Robert Gray, skipper of the
trading ship *Columbia* out of Boston. It was customary
for the British to gather pelts during the summer, then
sail to China in late fall, and Gray had been reasonably
successful trading northward from Vancouver Island
while the British were absent. But the winter of 1791-
92 was severe and most of the northern islets froze
solidly, forcing Gray to turn southward where sea otter
were less plentiful.

Poking into every inlet, though with little success,
Gray worked his way around Puget Sound and down
the Pacific coast. By May 10, 1792, he had reached
Cape Disappointment at the southern tip of Washing-

ton, having gathered only a few furs of poor quality. It had been known for more than ten years that a river of considerable size entered the Pacific at this point, but its mouth was barricaded by treacherous sand bars and high breakers which had blocked every attempt to cross them. Desperately in need of furs, Robert Gray determined to find a way across the barrier. Waiting for flood tide, at four o'clock on the morning of May 11, he sent a small boat ahead to take soundings, then followed cautiously with the *Columbia,* and soon found himself "in a large river of fresh water up which we entered."

Robert Gray had few peers as a sea captain and navigator, but his Yankee terseness and preoccupation with trade made him something less than a great explorer. He sailed only a few miles up the estuary, named the river for his ship, then anchored, and set about trading when "vast numbers of natives came alongside." The trade was brisk enough for him to complete his cargo in nine days, so he sailed away for China, though first rowing ashore to claim the entire watershed of the river as a possession of the United States. His matter-of-fact log shows that he changed anchorage once and that the water was ten fathoms deep, but gives no description of the land or the Indians, who had obviously never before seen white men. Fortunately, Gray had in his crew a seventeen-year-old boy, John Boit, who not only kept a journal but was highly observant, imaginative, and articulate. A few random sentences from his journal were of greater value than all the furs obtained in trade:

"The men at Columbia's River are strait limb'd, fine looking fellows, and the women are very pretty. They are all in a state of Nature except the Females, who wear a leaf Apron. The Indians are very numerous, and appear'd very civil (not even offering to steal). During our short stay we collected 150 Otter, 300 Beaver, and twice that number of land furs. The river abounds with excellent Salmon, and most other River fish, and the woods with plenty of Moose and Deer, the skins of which was brought us in great plenty.

"This River in my opinion, wou'd be a fine place to set up a Factory [a trading post]. We found plenty of Oak, Ash and Walnut trees, and clear ground in plenty, which with little labour might be made fit to raise such seeds as is necessary for the sustenance of inhabitants, and in short, a factory set up here and another at Hancock's River in the Queen Charlotte Isles, wou'd engross the whole trade of the NW Coast (with the help of a few small coasting vessels)."

LEWIS AND CLARK

Thomas Jefferson had never lost interest in John Ledyard's scheme for trapping the fur resources of the Northwest by way of a transcontinental water route. That interest was fanned to a flame by Gray's discovery of the Columbia River and John Boit's description of its advantages as an ideal place to locate a settlement, for Jefferson was an expansionist who had fully recognized the implications of the Nootka Sound Convention. Although not actually stated, the agreement made occupancy the basis of sovereignty in the Northwest, whether the settlers were British subjects or those of any other nation, and he believed the future security of the United States required possession of an outlet to the Pacific. Great Britain, however, had a much better opportunity to plant and supply settlements in the Northwest, since she already dominated the fur trade, and the distance by sea was no greater from London than from Boston. Furthermore, the claim of the United States to the Columbia watershed was obviously weak, since Gray had not explored the river above the estuary. But the French had explored and mapped the Missouri to its source at the Continental

Divide, and Jefferson was familiar with their maps. He reasoned correctly that, since the Columbia was a mighty river flowing into the Pacific from the east, its source must be contiguous to that of the Missouri, and that the two rivers would provide the transcontinental water route Ledyard had envisaged. If so, it would reduce the distance to less than one fifth that by sea, providing an inexpensive means of transporting and supplying settlers.

Jefferson was anxious that the United States should immediately strengthen its claim to the Columbia watershed by actual exploration, and that it should, if possible, discover a water route connecting the Pacific with the Mississippi Valley. As Secretary of State, he could take no official action that would trespass on the French territory lying between the Mississippi River and Continental Divide, but he prevailed upon the American Philosophical Society to finance an expedition to the Columbia by way of the Missouri "for scientific research." A fund was subscribed, but, due to fear of involvement in the war between France and England, the expedition was never launched.

When, in 1801, Jefferson became President of the United States, no American had explored the Columbia River more than a few miles above its estuary, but the huge sea-otter herds of the Northwest had been destroyed and inland furs were coming into great demand. In searching for them, the Hudson's Bay Company had for several years been pushing its trappers farther and farther to the westward, but it was unknown to Jefferson whether or not they had crossed the Continental Divide and explored the upper reaches of the Columbia. Still intent upon strengthening the claim of the United States to the Columbia watershed, he asked Congress for authority to send a small scientific expedition to explore the Missouri and Columbia rivers "for the purpose of acquiring knowledge of the geography, plants, and animals of the interior."

Before congressional action had been taken upon the President's request, it became necessary for the United States to make the Louisiana Purchase, acquiring from France all her territory between the Mississippi River and the Continental Divide. The purchase had no sooner been made than Jefferson again asked Congress to authorize an expedition, this time for the purpose of exploring the newly acquired territory. The authority was granted, and the President chose Meriwether Lewis, his personal secretary, to carry out the project; but it is obvious that the sole purpose of the expedition was for the exploration of the Columbia River and discovery of a transcontinental water route.

Lewis chose for his second-in-command Lieutenant William Clark, a brother of the famous American frontiersman George Rogers Clark. During the winter of 1903-4, Lewis and Clark assembled at St. Louis supplies for a two-year expedition, and enlisted a crew of about fifty men, made of young frontiersmen, soldiers, and French river men. On May 14, 1804, the explorers set out in a large keelboat and two pirogues, the soldiers riding along the banks to hunt game and ward off Indian attacks. Lewis carried French maps of the headwaters of the Missouri, but so little was known of the topography of the area that he took along wheels and axles for making the expected portage to the headwaters of the Columbia.

Progress was slow against the strong current of the Missouri, and winter had set in by the time the villages of the friendly Mandan Indians were reached, a short distance north of the present site of Bismarck, North Dakota. These villages were the frontier outpost, and for two or more generations had been visited by French traders and trappers. There Lewis and Clark made their winter camp, and met a shiftless French half-breed named Charbonneau whose eighteen-year-old Shoshoni wife, Sacagawea, had in childhood been stolen from her people in western Montana. Since no one in the

Lewis and Clark expedition was adept at sign language, communication threatened to be a greater barrier than the unknown wilderness to the west. But Sacagawea could speak various Indian languages and converse with Charbonneau, who could speak in barely distinguishable English. On the promise that he would be required to do no work, Charbonneau agreed to accompany the expedition as interpreter.

In the spring of 1805, Lewis sent the soldiers back to St. Louis with reports for President Jefferson. At the same time he and Clark started upstream in two pirogues and six canoes, taking with them twenty-six men, a French-Canadian guide, Lewis's servant, Charbonneau, and Sacagawea with her baby on a cradle board. By early June they had reached Great Falls, Montana, but were unable to continue with the pirogues, and were obliged to cache a large part of their supplies. Above the falls the guide knew nothing of the country, but Sacagawea began recognizing scenes of her childhood, and it was believed that people from her tribe would soon be found who could guide the party to the headwaters of the Columbia. The hope failed to materialize. No Indians of any tribe were encountered, portages had to be made with increasing frequency, and two months were required to ascend the Missouri to its headwaters at the Idaho-Montana boundary.

On August 12, the party scaled the Continental Divide and discovered a band of Indians well supplied with horses. Sacagawea ran to meet them with tears rolling down her cheeks, sucking her fingers to show the Americans that these were her relatives. They supplied the expedition with thirty-eight horses, and led it northward for several days, then refused to go farther. As far as Charbonneau was concerned, Sacagawea could have turned back with her people, but she had come to admire Clark greatly, and at his request decided to go on. For three weeks the explorers groped their way northward to a point near present Missoula,

Montana. Finding a well-worn Indian trail that led to the west, they followed it across the summit of the divide, then lost it among a jumble of barren black mountains. No game was found, the food supply became exhausted, and to stave off starvation the lost explorers were obliged to live on horse flesh. Staggering with exhaustion, they reached Clearwater River at the present site of Orofino, Idaho, in early October.

The valley of the Clearwater was green and fertile, hundreds of excellent horses grazed in the meadows, and a village of neat brush wickiups stood beside the stream. Friendly, intelligent Indians dressed in white buckskin came out to meet the famished explorers. They called themselves Nez Percés, welcomed the whites, and brought them roasted fish and bread made of camass-root flour. To questions translated by Scagawea, an old man told of having canoed down the river for "many suns to a great lake of salt water."

Lewis and Clark spent several days at the Nez Percé village, while the men regained strength, felled trees, and hollowed them into canoes. A council was held with the chiefs, and in exchange for two guns and a keg of powder the Indians agreed to care for the expedition's horses until it should return. On October 7, 1805, the Lewis and Clark expedition set off down the Clearwater in six log canoes. Exactly a month later, they heard the roar of the Pacific through the fog that shrouded the mouth of the Columbia River.

Lewis and Clark built Fort Clatsop on the south bank of the river, spent the winter uneventfully among the friendly Indians, and in late March of 1806 started their return journey. At the Nez Percé village they found their horses well cared for. The Indians were happy to see them, loaded their packs with dried meat and camass flour, and guided them by a good trail across the Continental Divide to the vicinity of Missoula. Before turning back, they pointed up the Blackfoot branch of Clark's Fork River as the best route to the great falls of the Missouri. Lewis, with half the men, took the proposed route, while Clark turned southward to explore the Yellowstone River and then rejoin Lewis at its confluence with the Missouri. He held roughly to the outcoming route until reaching Three Forks, then turned eastward to the Yellowstone at the present site of Livingston, Montana. His passage down the river was made without difficulty, and he encountered only friendly Indians.

The route over which the Nez Percés had led the explorers back to Missoula and the one pointed out along the Blackfoot were easily travelable and led in an almost straight line from the Clearwater to the great falls of the Missouri, forming a perfect link between the navigable portions of the two great river systems. As a result, Lewis was able to make the return journey in a quarter of the time required for the outgoing trip, and reached Great Falls far ahead of schedule. Delighted with the success of his expedition, and with time on his hands, he decided to explore the plains country to the north, and, in doing so, closed to Americans the transcontinental route that Jefferson had sent to discover.

From Great Falls, Lewis marched north to the Marias River, turned westward almost to the portals of present Glacier National Park, and had started back when he encountered a band of Blackfoot Indians. Whether or not the ensuing battle was avoidable, the Lewis party opened fire on the Indians and won the evrlasting hatred of the Blackfeet for all Americans. The Indians had long been in contact with the French-Canadian trappers of the Hudson's Bay Company, were well equipped with firearms, and their homeland was the territory surrounding the upper reaches of the Missouri and Yellowstone rivers. Since they were the most powerful and warlike tribe in the Northwest, their hatred closed both rivers to American travel.

Following his unfortunate battle wih the Blackfeet,

Lewis marched down the Teton River to the Missouri, built boats, and, as planned, met Clark at the confluence of the Yellowstone. Charbonneau, Sacagawea, and two of the men who had decided to stay on the frontier were left at the Mandan villages. The rest of the expedition floated rapidly down the Missouri and reached St. Louis on September 25, 1806.

As soon as Meriwether Lewis had sent off a report to President Jefferson, he and William Clark settled down to the serious business of editing their journals for publication. They were, however, a bit too painstaking, and did not complete the task for eight years. Sergeant Patrick Gass, one of their men, had also kept a journal, and Gass though less particular about the excellence of his prose, was more practical. He had his journal in the hands of a publisher within less than a year, and several editions were quickly sold, firing the American imagination as nothing before had ever done. Frontiersmen soon began poling keelboats far up the Missouri to trade gaudy, white man's good with the Indians for beaver pelts. The most ambitious of these was Manuel Lisa, forerunner of the Missouri Fur Company. One of his parties, under the command of Andrew Henry, worked its way far up the Yellowstone River where it was attacked by Blackfoot Indians. Henry and a few of his men escaped afoot, and were driven westward across the Continental Divide. On a branch of the Snake River, fifty miles west of Teton National Park, they built a log cabin and holed up for the winter. The cabin became known as Henry's Fort, the first American outpost on the western side of the Rockies.

THE ASTORIANS

The greatest effect of the Gass journal was upon the imagination of John Jacob Astor, who dominated the fur industry in the United States and whose clipper ships dominated the China trade. His only rivals were the British-controlled Hudson's Bay Company and the Scottish-controlled Northwest Fur Company, both of which had pushed their operations across Canada to the Pacific. From the journals of Patrick Gass and John Boit, Astor conceived a plan for outmaneuvering his two great rivals and gaining complete control of the fur industry in the Northwest.

In the last year of Jefferson's administration, Astor went to him with his plan. He proposed to establish trading posts at frequent intervals along the Missouri to the Rockies and down the Columbia to the Pacific. He would also build a large fortified headquarters post at the mouth of the Columbia, an ideal location from which to make shipments for the China trade. Furs from the upper Missouri and Columbia would be taken there cheaply and rapidly over the water route pioneered by Lewis and Clark. A fleet of small ships would ply along the Pacific coast from California to Alaska, circulating among the islands and up the rivers to trade for furs with the Indians. In this way Astor believed his rivals could be forced to abandon their operations in British Columbia. Jefferson was enthusiastic about the plan, seeing in it the possibility of gaining American sovereignty in the Northwest by developing industry there.

In June, 1810, the Pacific Fur Company was incorporated. The ship *Tonquin* was at once loaded with provisions, building materials, and trade goods at New York, and set sail for the mouth of the Columbia under the command of Alexander McKee. That fall Wilson Hunt set off from St. Louis with a large party of frontier trappers and river men, taking two barges and a keelboat heavily loaded with supplies, traps, and trade goods. They were to follow the Lewis and Clark route, trap the upper Missouri and Columbia, select sites for trading posts, and meet the *Tonquin* at the Columbia Estuary.

Hunt wintered at the present site of St. Joseph, Missouri. He had just started on, in the spring of 1811, when John Colter, one of the two members of the Lewis and Clark expedition who had remained at the Mandan villages, came down the river, nearly naked and on the verge of starvation. In 1807, he had gone back to the headwaters of the Missouri, discovered the area that later became Yellowstone National Park, and been captured by the Blackfeet. A month before his meeting with Hunt's party, Colter had made his escape and had ridden a tangle of driftwood fifteen hundred miles downstream on the spring freshet. He reported that the Blackfoot hatred for Americans was such that nothing short of an army could make its way through their homeland. There was only one way in which he believed the expedition could reach the headwaters of the Columbia. It would have to leave the Missouri at the Arikara village, located below the present site of Bismarck, and make its way overland, keeping well to the south of Blackfoot territory.

A few days later, Colter's opinion was confirmed by three Kentuckians who came paddling down the river. They had been in Andrew Henry's party that had been driven across the divide by the Blackfeet, and had made their way overland to the Arikara village. They were positive that the upper Missouri could not be traversed by Americans, but offered to guide the expedition overland to Henry's Fort, and assured Hunt that he could reach the Columbia from there by way of Snake River.

With little other choice open, Hunt engaged the Kentuckians as guides. The Arikara village was reached in mid-June, but the Indians were short of horses, and only eighty-two could be secured. These were loaded with trade goods, traps, and supplies, and, with the men afoot, the expedition set off across the prairies. The guides led the way to the point where North and South Dakota now meet at the Montana line. There they ad-

mitted they were lost, but were sure that Blackfoot territory lay nearby to the north. For two months the
party groped its way to the south and west through the
Wyoming mountains, while the men became footsore
and exhausted, supplies ran low, and horses died from
lack of forage. Then, from the top of a pass, the guides
recognized the towering peaks of the Teton Range,
and in early October led the weary expedition to
Henry's deserted fort.

After a day's rest, Hunt set his men to felling trees
and hollowing them into canoes. But now that a tributary of the Columbia had been reached, he decided to
start trapping operations. He assigned an ex-Army
officer, Joseph Miller, to make the abandoned fort his
headquarters. With the three guides who were familiar
with the area, Miller was to care for the horses and trap
beaver until spring, then bring his fur packs downstream to the main fort at the mouth of the Columbia.

By October 20, fifteen canoes had been completed,
were loaded with nearly five tons of trade goods, traps,
and provisions, and the expedition set off down the
Snake River. The current was swift, the canoes sped
along with little effort, the river men sang lustily, and
Hunt was equally joyful. Having lost so much time, he
had feared that winter might maroon them in the high
mountains, but at this rate of travel they should easily
reach the mouth of the Columbia in three or four
weeks.

The first difficulty was encountered at the rapids
above Idaho Falls where two days, a canoe, and a half
ton of trade goods were lost. They had two days of fast,
smooth travel past the mouth of the Portneuf River,
which flows into the Snake below the present location
of Pocatello. The American Falls was reached, and
below them the river swung away to the west, boiling
through a canyon that was chiseled deep between the
Snake River Plain and ranges of low, desolate mountains to the south. Only the amazing skill of the river

men kept the canoes from swamping in the maelstrom below the falls, and each day the gorge narrowed and deepened. On October 28, near the present site of Twin Falls, a canoe loaded with most of the provisions capsized; one man was drowned, and four were barely rescued. Hunt sent scouts along the canyon rim, but they returned to report that the river was entirely impassable, that the canoes would have to be abandoned.

The situation was clearly desperate. Only five days' rations remained, winter was setting in. It was too late to turn back to Henry's Fort, and nearly a thousand miles to the mouth of the Columbia. In order to travel as rapidly as possible, nothing could be carried except food, warm clothing, arms, and ammunition. Hunt had caches dug, the trade goods, traps, and even his own journal buried. For three weeks the men struggled down the north bank of the river, through barren country entirely devoid of game, and were kept alive only by the few Indians they found fishing along the stream. In late November they reached the mouth of the Boise River, where the Snake turns northward through an awesome canyon to form the boundary between Oregon and Idaho. There Indians were found with a fair supply of scrawny horses, but Hunt's party had little to trade for them. They obtained a few, butchered one, and continued northward along the canyon rim.

Unable to travel more than a mile or two a day in their weakened condition, Hunt and his men reached the mouth of the Weiser River on Christmas Day. There they found a little village of friendly Shoshoni Indians, but their food supply for the winter consisted of only a few dogs and a small herd of emaciated horses. Regardless of their own poverty they took in the destitute whites and butchered horses and dogs to feed them. From these Indians, Hunt learned that the Columbia could be reached in winter only by crossing the Snake and following old Indian trails for twenty-one sleeps to the northwest. But with snow already deep, the trails could be followed only by Indians who were thoroughly familiar with the route. In exchange for a gun, a pistol, a few knives, and a little ammunition, the Indians agreed to furnish guides, five horses for food, and to care until spring for the men who were too weak to travel.

Three days were required for the strongest of the party to descend the Snake River canyon, cross the swift stream in a horsehide canoe, and climb out to the western rim. Then the guides led them to the northwest, the first white men to travel any part of the route that would become the Oregon Trail. The Indians turned up the canyon of Burnt River, skirted the eastern foothills of the Blue Mountains past the present site of Baker, Oregon, and continued northwest into the fertile valley of the Grande Ronde. There a few more horses were obtained at a Shoshoni village and new guides secured. These led the way across the forest-covered Blue Mountains and down to the present location of Pendleton on the Umatilla River. The Cayuse Indians in the Umatilla Valley were prosperous and generous. Hundreds of horses grazed in the meadows, and the lodges were well supplied with dried buffalo meat and camass-root flour. For five days the half-starved whites rested with the Indians, feasting and regaining their strength. When they went on, they were well mounted and supplied with provisions. At The Dalles, Hunt traded his horses for canoes, and on February 15, 1812, he and his party, saved only by the generosity of Indians, reached Fort Astoria on the Columbia Estuary.

The sea division of the Astor enterprise had fared little better than the overland party. At first all had gone well. For Astoria was built, and the *Tonquin* sailed northward to trade for furs at Nootka Sound, but the Indians, cheated and abused by other white traders, swarmed aboard. Most of the crew, including Alexander McKee, were massacred, and the remainder trapped in the hold of the vessel. Having no possibility of escape, they blew up the powder magazine, killing all hands and sinking the ship with its cargo of trade goods.

Loss of the trade goods in the *Tonquin,* in addition to those cached by the overland party, left the Pacific Fur Company in a desperate situation. Hunt decided to send a report of the double tragedy to Astor as quickly as possible. Six couriers, under the leadership of twenty-year-old Robert Stuart, were started off in the late spring of 1812. Stuart's instructions were to follow Snake River to the caches, retrieve Hunt's journal, and make his way to St. Louis by the shortest possible route.

ROBERT STUART ON
THE BIG MEDICINE TRAIL

Robert Stuart, though young, was a natural frontiersman. He ascended the Columbia by canoe, traded with the Cayuse Indians for twenty horses, and had no difficulty in following well-worn Indian trails across northwestern Oregon to the Snake River. He kept to the west side of the canyon until he found an easy crossing place opposite the mouth of the Boise River, followed that stream eastward past the present site of Boise, Idaho, then turned southeast over the desert to the lower bend of the Snake. He had barely reached the river when he found Joseph Miller and the three Kentuckians whom Hunt had left at Henry's Fort the previous fall. Their trapping had been amazingly successful. They had twice gathered beaver pelts worth several thousand dollars, but both times had been robbed by Crow Indians, and were trying to make their way to the Columbia. All four had become disgusted with fur trapping, and decided to accompany Stuart to St. Louis.

Unprofitable as Miller's trapping had been, it was

of great importance to the history of the West, for in
his wandering he had discovered one of the key links
of the Oregon Trail. After reaching the caches, Miller
led Stuart along the Snake to the Portneuf River, southward up its valley where Pocatello now stands, over a
low divide, and down to the broad green valley of Bear
River. Near the southeast corner of Idaho, the couriers
were attacked by a war party of Crow Indians, and
driven to the north along the present Wyoming-Idaho
boundary. Stuart and his men rode at the limit of their
horses' endurance for sixty miles or more. Then, believing themselves out of danger, they made camp and
turned the jaded horses out to graze. At dawn, next
morning, the Crows swooped down upon the camp
in a whooping, shrieking attack, plundered it, and drove
the horses away. Afoot, Stuart had little choice but to
strike out for Henry's Fort, hoping to find there some
of the horses left by Hunt the previous fall. A month
was lost before the half-starved party made its way to
the abandoned fort, only to find that the horses had all
been stolen or had drifted away.

For several days the couriers stayed with the Indians,
resting and regaining their strength. Their only means
of communication was sign language, but Stuart was
adept at it. When he asked for directions to a pass at
the north end of the Wind River Mountains, the Indians
made signs that the snow would be too deep for a crossing. One of them scratched an outline of the range on
the ground, drew a mark around its southern end, and
made gestures to indicate a broad, low pass that would
be free of snow.

For an ax, a pistol, and a little ammunition, the
Indians sold Stuart a thin old horse and a six-day supply of dried buffalo meat. On October 19 the couriers
set out toward the southeast and, with their strength
restored, traveled rapidly on short rations. Half their
meat supply was still left when they reached the southern end of the Wind River Range, about a hundred

miles due east of the point at which they had been
turned northward by the Crow attack. The mountains
flattened into a series of low hills, rising gently to the
eastern horizon, and a deeply worn Indian trail led
over them. There could be no doubt that this was the
southern pass the Snake Indians had indicated. Stuart
turned toward it, crossed the Continental Divide without realizing it, and came down to the Sweetwater
River, flowing to the east.

In the valley of the Sweetwater, the couriers found
game plentiful, and made their way downstream to the
North Platte without difficulty. Near Red Buttes, a few
miles above the present site of Casper, Wyoming, Stuart
found a nook in the mountains that was surrounded by
cedars and protected from winter storms. Mountain
sheep and deer wintered in the valley, and buffalo
were plentiful on the flatlands below. The couriers built
a log cabin among the cedars and wintered comfortably.
In the spring of 1813, they continued their journey
down the Platte to the Missouri afoot, and on to St.
Louis by canoe.

With the exception of a hundred-mile gap between
Bear River and South Pass, Stuart had blazed the
route that would become the general course of the
Overland Trail, and was fully aware that he had discovered the most direct overland route to the Columbia.
He painstakingly wrote a report of his journey and the
exact route taken, noting that most of the distance
could be traveled by wheeled vehicles. But his report
received little attention, for in the War of 1812 the
British had gained complete control of the Columbia
River. Astor sold what remained of the Pacific Fur
Company to his rivals, and for six years the Columbia
was closed to Americans. By the time the treaty of
1818 was negotiated, again opening the Oregon region
to settlement by citizens of the United States, Stuart's
report and the route he pioneered had been nearly for-
gotten.

THE MOUNTAIN MEN

The general peneration of the Rockies by Americans was set off by the success of Ashley's first beaver-trapping venture. When, in the fall of 1822, his fur packs worth $24,000 were returned to St. Louis, hundreds of frontiersmen rushed to the mountains, most of them by keelboat up the Missouri River. Of all the hundreds, those to become most famous in pushing the American frontier westward were among the Ashley men: Jedediah Smith, Tom Fitzpatrick, Jim Bridger, and the Sublettes—William and Milton—to be joined later by Kit Carson.

In the fall of 1823, Smith and Fitzpatrick led their bands southward from the Yellowstone, trapping the Big Horn River and its tributaries. By midwinter their fur packs were bulging and they had reached the headwaters of the Big Horn in west-central Wyoming, where the beaver streams were frozen solidly. To return to the Yellowstone would require a trek of more than three hundred miles, the furs could not be boated to St. Louis until the ice went out of the upper Missouri in late spring, and in the meantime there would be great danger of losing them to the Blackfeet. So as to reduce the danger as much as possible, the trappers decided to pitch their winter camp well to the south of Blackfoot territory, and make their return to the Yellowstone in early spring. In search of a location with abundant game, they crossed a low divide and reached the Sweetwater less than fifty miles east of South Pass.

Smith reasoned that since the Sweetwater flowed to the east it must be a tributary of the Platte. If so, it should provide a short cut of seven or eight hundred miles to St. Louis, over which fur packs could be canoed, and which would entirely avoid danger from the Blackfeet. He and Fitzpatrick decided to cache their furs until spring, and explore what they believed to be completely unknown country to the west. They turned up the Sweetwater and crossed the Continental Divide by way of the age-old Indian trail, thus gaining credit as the discoverers of South Pass, since few historians knew of Robert Stuart's discovery in 1812. On the west side of the pass they followed Pacific and Sandy creeks down to the Green River, pioneering a section of the Oregon Trail which Stuart had not traveled. At the Green they separated to trap independently, agreeing to meet the following June at the cache buried on the Sweetwater. Their take of beaver pelts during the spring of 1824 was far beyond expectation, and their meeting at the cache made history as the first rendezvous held in the Rockies.

At the rendezvous it was decided that Fitzpatrick with a few men should take the fur packs to St. Louis, and return to the present site of Green River, Wyoming, with supplies for the following season. In the meantime, Smith and the balance of the men would hunt out the other Ashley trapping bands and guide them to the beaver-rich territory which is now western Wyoming.

A large buffalo-hide canoe was fashioned, loaded with pelts worth $30,000, and Fitzpatrick set off down the Sweetwater in late June. The stream was in freshet from melting snows, the heavily loaded canoe barely manageable among the submerged boulders, and on July 4 it was wrecked at a point where a great dome of rock stood in a meadow beside the Sweetwater. Fur packs bobbed away like corks on the racing water, part of them were lost, and the remainder saved only at the reckless risk of the men's lives.

Fitzpatrick realized that transporting valuable fur packs by canoe would be too hazardous until the rivers had been thoroughly explored. Because of the date, he named the dome Independence Rock, dug caches at its base, and buried the salvaged furs. To make the exploration he fashioned another canoe, but it was wrecked within thirty miles, at Fiery Narrows below the

confluence of the Sweetwater and Platte. This time the
men barely escaped with their lives, and lost most of
their guns and ammunition. Having nothing to trade
with the Indians for horses, Fitzpatrick and his men
made their way afoot along the Platte to the prairies of
western Nebraska. There the river, after being joined
by the South Platte, became nearly a mile wide, but
was too shallow for heavily loaded canoes. As a navigable water route, the Platte-Sweetwater system had
proved to be impracticable. But its course to the central
Rockies was little more than half the distance of that
by way of the upper Missouri, and, like Stuart, Fitzpatrick believed the entire route could be traveled by
wheeled vehicles. He reached Fort Atkinson, near the
present site of Council Bluffs, in early September,
obtained pack horses on Ashley's credit, and returned
with the fur packs in late October.

By November, Fitzpatrick had delivered the fur packs
to St. Louis, told General Ashley of the rich fur country discovered beyond the Continental Divide, and
urged him to transport supplies for the next season by
wagon train. The general realized that wagon transportation would be far less expensive than the use of
pack horses, but would not take the risk until he had
assured himself of its practicability. With Fitzpatrick he
took one wagon and two sets of harness to Fort Atkinson by keelboat, and set out for the mountains in
late November, taking along twenty-five men, fifty pack
horses loaded with supplies, and the wagon, drawn by
four stout mules. Keeping to the south side of the
Platte, and with the ground frozen solid, he had no
difficulty until reaching the mountains in eastern Wyoming. From there on the wagon was a handicap, since
the trail often had to be widened to allow passage, or
detours made around gulches that could be easily
crossed by pack animals. The experiment, however,
proved that wagons could be taken over the route, and

newspapers throughout the East ran glowing accounts of the first wheeled vehicle ever to be taken across the Continental Divide.

The bringing of a wagon to the heart of the beaver country was of no interest to the mountain men. But bringing supplies and taking back fur packs was of tremendous importance, for it saved each trapper band a four-thousand-mile round trip to St. Louis. The success of the 1825 rendezvous was so great that one was held every summer for the next decade and a half, usually in far-western Wyoming, and the route along the Sweetwater and Platte became the thoroughfare to and from civilization.

Within a few years the American mountain men had learned every stream and pass in the Rockies, as far west as central Idaho. Jim Bridger had built his famous fort in the southwestern corner of Wyoming, and had pushed westward through the Uinta Mountains to discover Great Salt Lake. Fitzpatrick had trapped every tributary of the Green River; Carson had penetrated far into the dangerous Blackfoot country of western Montana; and Jed Smith had bridged the remainder of the gap in the Oregon Trail left open by Robert Stuart. From Fort Bridger he had worked his way up Black Fork Creek to present Granger, Wyoming, then continued up Ham's Fork to its source near the Wyoming-Idaho boundary. From there he crossed a low ridge to the west, reached Bear River at about the point where Stuart was turned north by the Crow attack, and descended the Portneuf to trap the headwater of Snake River. While the American trappers were pushing their way to the northwest, the Hudson's Bay Company was pushing its men farther and farther to the southeast from the Columbia. By 1830 the entire route which would become the Oregon Trail was as well known to white men as it had been to the Indians when it was their Big Medicine Trail.

4

The Oregon Trail

THE IMMIGRANTS

Hall J. Kelley was a Boston schoolmaster with a deep-rooted hatred of the British. Following the renewal, in 1827, of the treaty which opened the Northwest to settlement by citizens of the United States, he began bombarding Congress with demands that troops be sent to "drive out the British tyrants." When his demands were ignored, he circulated thousands of pamphlets, urging New England farmers to gather at Boston with their families and household goods to join him in migrating overland to Oregon, a region of "unparalleled advantages." Kelley had, very evidently, read Robert Stuart's report of discovering the Sweetwater-Platte route, Lewis and Clark's journal, and newspaper accounts of Ashley's taking a wagon over the Continental Divide. Selecting the most glowing portions of these, he added to them from his own fertile imagination, producing an Oregon that would have put the Garden of Eden to shame, and describing the broad highway leading to it through a land of abundance. The entire journey could easily be made in carriages, "by way of a depression in the Rocky Mountains." All the Indians of the West were friendly and generous, so the passage was perfectly safe for women and children, and there was no need to take along provisions, since the fertile plains were "teeming with buffalo."

No New Englanders left their rocky farms to journey with schoolmaster Kelley to the Promised Land, but his pamphlet aroused the interest of a most unusual man: twenty-eight-year-old Nathaniel Wyeth. Imaginative, venturesome, forceful, and practical, Wyeth had already established himself as a successful businessman, cutting ice from ponds near Boston and shipping it to the West Indies. He hunted out and studied the Lewis and Clark journal, Gass's diary, available records of the Hudson's Bay Company, Robert Stuart's report, and newspaper articles regarding the exploits of the American mountain men. From these he gained a fairly good understanding of the difficulties to be encountered in crossing the continent, and realized that Kelley's scheme was simply a visionary's dream. He had no interest in driving out the British, but was much intrigued with the prospects of Oregon, and wrote in his journal, "I cannot divest myself of the opinion that I shall compete better with my fellow men in new and untried paths than in those to pursue which requires only patience and attention."

When Kelley's colonization plan failed to materialize, Wyeth decided to carry out the venture himself, but in a practical manner. He announced that he would enlist as many as fifty sturdy, single young men for the expedition, each of whom must have a trade, a profession, or be a successful farmer. Instead of representing the cross-country journey as Kelley had, Wyeth stressed its ruggedness and danger. To prepare for it, the men would be given three months' training on an island in Boston Harbor, where they would be toughened and taught frontiersmanship. He would arrange to finance the venture, and would send a ship ahead to the Columbia River, loaded with supplies, seed, cattle, and farming equipment. But each man would be required to sign a contract for his share of the investment, to be repaid over a period of five years from his farming profits after reaching Oregon.

Wyeth had no illusions about driving wagons and carriages from Boston to Oregon. He would send his wagons by ship and transport his expedition to St. Louis on canal barges and river packets, which were already in operation. Although the route from St. Louis followed rivers for nearly the entire distance, he understood that they were not always navigable, but his ingenious mind devised a means which he believed would overcome the difficulty. He invented and drew plans for a keelboat mounted on sturdy wheels.

The cost of chartering a ship to sail around Cape Horn would be great, but Wyeth conceived a plan for meeting the expense. From his study he had learned of the great demand for trade goods by the Indians of the Northwest, and the ship could fill out its cargo with such goods, on which a handsome profit should be made. With his well-laid plans and reputation as a successful businessman, Wyeth had no difficulty in raising whatever funds he could not supply himself. They were furnished by three Boston merchants, upon the agreement that they would share in the profits from the trade goods. His financing amply assured, Wyeth set about preparing for the undertaking, but Yankees were reluctant to join so hazardous an adventure, and only twenty-four enlisted. They included Nathaniel's brother Dr. Jacob Wyeth, geologist John Ball, a gunsmith, a blacksmith, two carpenters, two fishermen, and sixteen hardy young farmers.

By early March, 1832, three wagon-boats had been built, the men trained, and a small sailing vessel started on its voyage, loaded with implements, supplies, seed, a few milch cows, and a large cargo of trade goods. Wyeth and his party left Boston on March 11, and reached St. Louis on April 18. Upon arrival, he learned that William Sublette was in town, preparing to take a hundred-horse caravan of supplies to the summer rendezvous at Pierre's Hole, near Henry's deserted fort on the headwaters of Snake River.

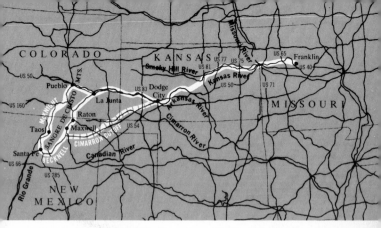

The Santa Fe Trail: routes of Robert McKnight and William Becknell opened trade to Santa Fe and then pioneered the Cimarron Cutoff, taking the first wagons over the trail. He was called "Father of the Santa Fe Trail."

Area of the Northwest Fur Trade. Captain James Cook's accidental discovery of Nootka Sound and his reception by fur-laden Indians opened a sea-otter fur trade in the Northwest.

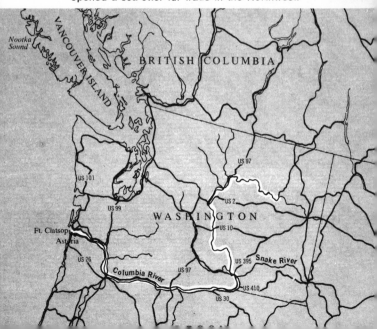

The Big Medicine Trail: the Lewis and Clark expedition. Although this was the natural route to the Northwest, Lewis's encounter with the Blackfoot Indians closed it off before it was really opened. Most of it remained undeveloped.

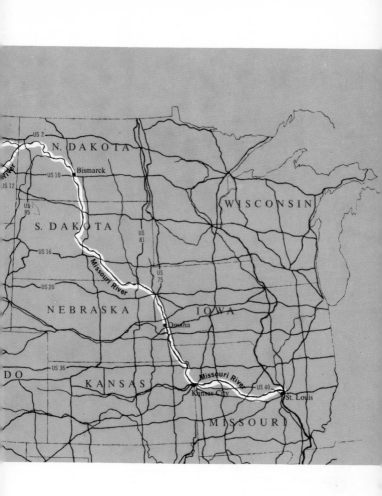

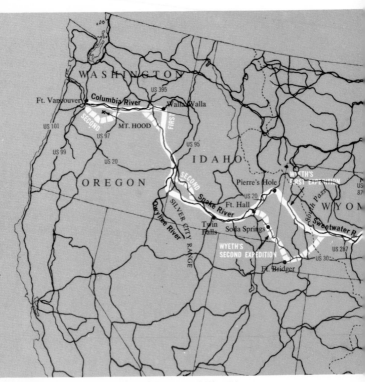

The Oregon Trail: routes of Nathaniel Wyeth's two immigrant parties, the first to reach Oregon. Their trail became the main route.

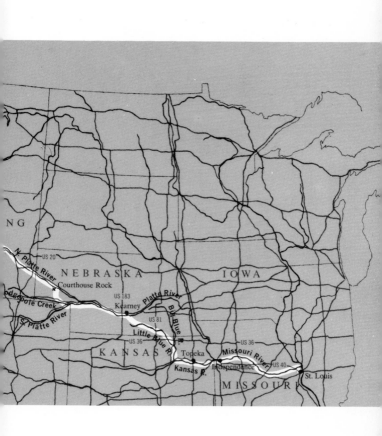

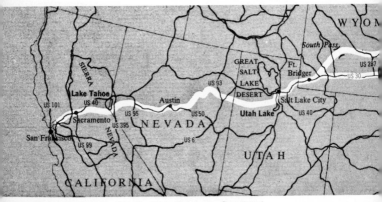

The California Trail: the Central Overland
Stage and Pony Express routes. The comple-
tion of first the telegraph and then the transcontinental railroad put an end to these color-
ful but hardly profitable ventures.

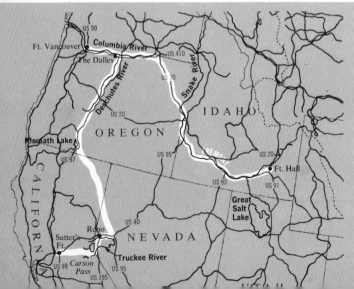

The Oregon Trail: William Sublette's cutoff route. He pioneered this shorter route while escorting Wyeth's first immigrant party.

The California Trail: John Frémont's expedition in search of a shorter route. He failed, but his report inspired many people to emigrate to California.

Wyeth hunted out Sublette, gained his goodwill, and asked to join his party to the caravan. Sublette agreed, but insisted that the wagon-boats be abandoned, pointing out that they would be too heavy to haul over rugged trails and too cumbersome to handle in rapid streams. Furthermore, Sublette was planning to take a cutoff route to the mountains. He would leave the Missouri at Independence, follow the Santa Fe Trail to the vicinity of present Topeka, Kansas, then strike northwest to reach the Platte.

Wyeth had taken great pride in his wagon-boats, but he sold them for half their cost and took a packet to Independence, where he secured horses for pack animals and mounting his men. Independence was then a rough, tough frontier town, thronged with carousing mountain men, painted Indians, and cursing teamsters waiting to drive the spring caravan over the Santa Fe Trail. It was enough to frighten three of Wyeth's recruits into quitting the expedition and turning back. In early May, the rest set off with Sublette's caravan to pioneer the route which became the main line of the Oregon Trail between Independence and the Platte River. Sublette crossed the Kansas River west of Topeka, turned northward along the Big Blue for some forty miles, then followed the Little Blue to its headwaters near Hastings, Nebraska, and came down to the wide valley of the Platte, opposite the present site of Kearney. There a war party of Pawnees overtook and passed the caravan, proudly waving a few bloody scalps just lifted from their enemies, the Kansas Indians. That was enough for three more of Wyeth's farmers. They set off down the Platte for St. Louis and home.

For twenty-seven days the combined caravan plodded westward along the south bank of the Platte, the Yankees continually amazed by the endless herds of buffalo that grazed along the valley. To avoid quicksand at the confluence, Sublette turned up the South Platte to the extreme northeast corner of Colorado, and followed Lodgepole Creek westward for about thirty miles. Then he turned north across a high divide, later known as Thirty-Mile Ridge, and reached the North Platte just below Courthouse Rock. This route also became the main line of the Oregon Trail, and Courthouse Rock one of its most famous landmarks. The trail from there so South Pass was that followed by both Stuart and Fitzpatrick, along the North Platte and Sweetwater. When the pass had been crossed, Sublette gave Wyeth his choice of going on with the caravan or striking out for Oregon by following the plainly marked trappers' trails southwest to Bridger's Fort, then turning northwest to the Bear, the Portneuf, and the Snake. The route Sublette described was to become the general course of the Oregon Trail, but Wyeth chose to continue with the rendezvous caravan.

Each year the mountain men's rendezvous had grown in size and dissipation, and that of 1832 was one of the largest and wildest. In mid-July the caravan reached Pierre's Hole, and the New Englanders were appalled at the stark barbarism of the scene. If this were a sample of the Far West, seven of Wyeth's men decided they wanted no more of it; they would return to St. Louis with William Sublette when he took back the fur packs. Wyeth, with the remaining eleven, joined Milton Sublette, who was leading a band of twenty men far down the Snake River to trap back upstream during late fall. Milton accompanied them to the vicinity of Twin Falls, Idaho, where he turned back, telling Wyeth to follow the river to its great canyon, then take any of the well-traveled Indian trails leading to the northwest.

Milton Sublette may have been unfamiliar with the Snake below Twin Falls, or may have neglected to tell Wyeth to cross to the north side after traveling some fifty or sixty miles. In any event, the Wyeth party kept to the south side of the river, where the terrain was broken by impassable gorges and canyons. Forced to leave the stream, they became lost in the mountains, ran out of provisions, and nearly starved before stumbling onto a village of friendly Shoshoni Indians on the Owyhee River of eastern Oregon. These Indians supplied them with dried salmon in exchange for a few fishhooks and trinkets, then guided them downstream to the Snake, and set them off on the age-old trail to the Columbia.

The trail was easily followed, but no Indians, either friendly or unfriendly, were found, and the Wyeth party was forced to live on horse meat. Instead of following the Umatilla River down to the Columbia, they continued northward on the Indian trail, and reached the present location of Walla Walla, Washington, on September 18, exhausted, ragged, and nearly starved. There they found a Hudson's Bay Company trading post. The agent received them with all hospitality, fed them, supplied them with new clothing, and traded their worn-out horses for provisions and a river barge. On October 29, the barge drew up at the Hudson's Bay Company dock at Fort Vancouver, bringing the first American immigrants to Oregon.

The factor at Fort Vancouver, Dr. John McLoughlin, welcomed Wyeth cordially, but gave him news that was far from welcome. The ship sent around Cape Horn had been lost at sea, leaving Wyeth nearly bankrupt and his little colony with no equipment, livestock, provisions, or supplies. Many men would have despaired, but Nat Wyeth was not the despairing type. He determined to raise additional capital, recruit more colonists, and organize another expedition as soon as possible. Always resourceful, he believed he knew how it could be done. Dried salmon would sell for ten cents a pound in Boston, but, during the spring salmon run, any quantity of it could be secured from Indians along the Columbia in exchange for a few fishooks and trinkets. The profit on a shipload would not only cover the cost of charter but pay for a cargo of farming equipment and supplies. Futhermore, rendezvous trade goods were worth four times as much in the mountains as at Boston, due to the labor cost of transporting them. If he could recruit a large party of colonists, the transportation of trade goods would cost practically nothing, and the profit would pay the expenses of the overland ourney.

In early February, 1833, Wyeth set out for Boston alone, met Milton Sublette on the Green River, and outlined his plan for bringing trade goods from Boston. Sublette agreed to buy three thousand dollars' worth, but only if they were delivered to Fort Bridger in time for the opening of the 1834 rendezvous.

Wyeth reached Boston in the late fall of 1833. The news that he had taken the remnant of his first expedition through safely to Oregon aroused great enthusiasm, particularly among the Methodists, who had long been anxious to plant missionaries among the heathen Indians of the Far West. The backers of the first venture, who had lost their entire investment, were far from enthusiastic, but Henry Hall, a Boston capitalist, agreed to finance a second venture. The brig *May Dacre* was chartered, loaded, and sailed for the Columbia in early winter. On February 7, 1834, Wyeth left Boston on his second colonizing expedition, taking with him rendezvous trade goods costing $800. There is no record of the exact number in his party, but it was far larger than the first. Among its members were two scientists, and several Methodist missionaries under the leadership of Jason Lee.

As before, Wyeth secured transportation to Independence by canal barge and river packet. The trade goods, camping gear, supplies, and provisions were loaded onto pack horses, and the colonists set out over the route taken on the previous expedition. But the start was made earlier in the spring, the weather was bad, and winter snows had been deep throughout the Rockies and Great Plains. The mud was deep, creeks and rivers overflowed their banks, and a day seldom passed without rain. Day after day was lost in waiting for streams to subside enough to be forded, and on many days no more than two or three miles could be traveled through the deep mud. The result was that Wyeth failed to reach Fort Bridger until the rendezvous was disbanding, and Milton Sublette refused to accept the trade goods.

Nat Wyeth was no man to grieve over adversities but quick to grasp and advantage, and he believed he had one. The first trader to arrive at rendezvous with his goods was assured of the greatest profit, and he planned to be first on the scene in 1835. He continued toward Oregon by the trappers' trail—up Bear River to Soda Springs, and down the Portneuf to the Snake. Ten miles north of Pocatello's present location, he set his colonists to building a stout log fort, which he named Fort Hall in honor of his backer. There he stored his trade goods, easily available to any rendezvous site along the Green River. Leaving a crew of twelve men to guard the merchandise and trap during the fall and spring seasons, he and the remainder of his colonists pushed on for the Columbia. They followed the trail pioneered by Stuart until reaching the river, then blazed the route which would become the Oregon Trail to the present site of Portland. It lay along the south side of the Columbia to The Dalles, then turned away from the river to circle Mount Hood and reach the Willamette Valley opposite Fort Vancouver.

Wyeth again found his hopes frustrated. The *May Dacre* had been struck by lighting at sea, and help up so long in making repairs that it missed the salmon run. Again his venture had been a financial failure, but he had opened the gateway of overland immigration to the Northwest, and it would never again be closed. He established his colony on an island at the mouth of the Willamette River; it prospered, and with each succeeding year more Americans arrived to clear farms and build homes farther up the valley.

THE MISSIONARIES

When the Methodists sent their missionaries west with Wyeth's second expedition, the American Board of Foreign Missions, supported by the Presbyterians and Congregationalists, bestirred itself immediately. At its convention in Ithaca, New York, it voted to send a party of six to the Columbia River Valley—two missionaries, their wives, a farmer, and a mechanic. Marcus Whitman, recently graduated from Fairfield Medical School, applied for one of the missionary posts, but he was, unfortunately, single. Twenty-six-year-old Narcissa Prentiss, pretty, vivacious, deeply religious, and ideally talented for a frontier missionary's wife, virtually threw herself into Whitman's arms, and made him eligible for the post by marrying him. As a second couple, the Board chose Reverend Henry Spalding and his fragile, ineffectual wife, Eliza.

The Whitmans, Spaldings, a farmer, and a carpenter traveled to St. Louis during the winter of 1835-36, and outfitted there. By prearrangement, they were to join a rendezvous supply caravan led by Tom Fitzpatrick, which was to assemble at Belleview, a little frontier settlement near the confluence of the Platte and Missouri. Like most of the immigrants who followed them in later years, the Whitmans and Spaldings outfitted far too heavily. In addition to household furniture, trunks of clothing, boxes of religious books, provisions for several months, and elaborate camping equipment, they bought two wagons, fourteen horses, six pack mules, and seventeen cattle—most of them milch cows. In mid-May of 1836, they boarded a packet and traveled up the Missouri to Belleview.

The Fitzpatrick caravan of 1836 was one of the strangest ever to set off for the Rockies. The main body was made up of four hundred pack animals and seventy frontiersmen—rough, tough American mountain men,

French-Canadian trappers, and Indian half-breeds. In ludicrous contrast was Sir William Drummond Stuart and his party of British sportsmen, bound for a "rousing buffalo hunt" on the prairies. The sportsmen were accompanied by an array of menservants, gunbearers, and dogs, and traveled in several ornate wagons, each drawn by six mules in glittering harness. To complete the motley assemblage, the missionaries trailed along behind, driving their milch cows and a few bawling calves.

At the outset the women were not only a curiosity to Fitzpatrick's rough crew but the object of more than a little ribald banter. Sister Spalding was shocked and appalled, but Narcissa Whitman glowed with exhilaration at the exciting adventure before her. A country judge's daughter, she was not unused to the profanity and rough talk of the frontiersmen, and showed no resentment of it. After a few days she won the admiration of the entire crew, and—within the limits of their ability and provocation—they watched their language in her presence. Whenever game was killed, the choicest cuts were brought to her tent, and the bearer's canteen was always filled with fresh milk.

The winter had been mild, the spring fairly dry, and travel was rather easy until the South Platte had been crossed. There the land began rising steeply toward the foothills of the Rockies. The wagons lagged behind, and, to cross Thirty-Mile Ridge, Whitman was obliged to jettison the least needed articles of furniture. Beyond Scotts Bluff the road became increasingly rugged. Long detours often had to be made around impassable gulches near the river, the draft animals weakened from overwork, and equipment which had seemed indispensable had to be discarded.

At Fort Laramie the British sportsmen left the caravan, and Fitzpatrick advised Whitman to abandon his wagons, transferring his goods to pack animals for the remainder of the journey. Whitman refused. If Ashley could cross the Continental Divide with a wagon, certainly a Christian gentleman could do the same. He had made up his mind to take his wagons through to the Columbia, and would not be deterred from his purpose. Fitzpatrick pointed out that there was no road, and that Ashley had been able to get his wagon through only by having a large crew and building road where necessary. Whitman finally agreed to leave one wagon, but was adamant about the other.

Beyond Fort Laramie the trail became more rugged as it ascended the eastern slope of the Rockies. Pack animals could easily climb it at the rate of two or three miles an hour, but it was unfit for wagon travel. Trees had to be cut, boulders pried aside, and detours made around deep gulches. Often the wagon tipped over two or three times in a single day, and most of the load had to be thrown out or transferred to pack animals, but Whitman was as stubborn as impractical. While Narcissa and the Spaldings rode with the caravan, he and the unfortunate farmer and carpenter fought the almost empty wagon up the valleys of the Platte and Sweetwater, and over South Pass to Bridger's Fort.

At the rendezvous the white women were as great an object of curiosity as they had been when first joining the caravan, and Narcissa made friends just as quickly. The mountain men, many of whom had not seen a white woman for several years, were fascinated by her beauty, and the Indians almost worshiped her. The squaws gathered in a throng, to touch their fingers to her white skin, marvel at her blue eyes, and admire her clothing.

Fortunately, Nathaniel Wyeth, after selling Fort Hall to the Hudson's Bay Company, had come to the rendezvous. Thomas McKay, adopted son of Dr. McLoughlin, was still at the fort, but would soon be returning to Walla Walla with a caravan. Wyeth gave Whitman a letter of introduction to McKay, and assured him that he could accompany the caravan to Oregon if he arrived at the fort in time, but urged that he abandon his wagon. Again Whitman refused, saying that if necessary he would make the journey unescorted: he had promised himself to open a road to the Columbia, and the wagon was going through. He was mistaken. By the time he reached Soda Springs, his draft animals were too exhausted to pull it farther.

Still determined to open a roadway to Oregon, Whitman discarded rear wheels and body, mounted a box on the front axle, and continued down the Portneuf to Fort Hall. The missionaries, nearly as exhausted as their draft animals, reached the fort just as McKay was setting out for Walla Walla. He welcomed them cordially, laid over a few days so they might rest and recuperate, then led the way down the south rim of Snake River Gorge. The caravan was continually slowed by the lumbering, makeshift cart, and at what is now Glenn's Ferry four mules were nearly drowned when the wheels capsized and tangled them in the harness.

McKay was thoroughly disgusted when Whitman insisted on going on with the useless cart. He wanted to be hospitable, but had lost all the time he could afford. Leaving three men for guides, he and his party rode away toward the Boise Basin. At the mouth of the Boise the guides also rebelled, threatening to leave the missionaries before trying to get the wheels across the Snake again. Whitman had no choice but to abandon his beloved vehicle and his ambition to open a wagon road to the Columbia. It was a sad disappointment, but also a great achievement, for he had proved that with no great amount of road-building the route was feasible for wagon travel.

Without the cumbersome vehicle, the party moved on at a good pace. On September 1, 1836, the first white women ever to have crossed the Rockies reached Fort Walla Walla, both in good health, and in barely more than three months from the time they had left the Missouri. Scarcely a month later, with help from the

Hudson's Bay Company, the Whitmans and Spaldings had constructed buildings and established missions among the Nez Percé Indians, twenty miles farther up the Walla Walla Valley.

Yankee ships plied regularly between Boston and the Pacific coast, trading for hides and tallow at the Spanish ports in California, and captains often sailed up the Columbia for furs and dried salmon. No ship returned without a packet of letters from the American missionaries and colonists, but particularly from Narcissa Whitman, extolling the wonders of Oregon and the ease and safety of the overland journey. Marcus Whitman sent off voluminous reports to the Board of Foreign Missions, urging that more missionaries and colonists be sent and boasting that he had opened a wagon road to "the very shore of Oregon." He, however, failed to mention that it was the Snake River shore, nearly four hundred miles short of Fort Vancouver.

These letters and reports created great enthusiasm in New England church circles. Each spring an increasing number of small emigrant wagon trains plodded westward from Independence, over the route which had become known as the Oregon Trail. As each train passed, the roughest stretches along the rails were improved: chutes cut into gulch banks, boulders rolled aside, wider openings slashed through woods and thickets, and the roadway along steep hillsides leveled enough so that wagons would not tip over. By 1839 a very passable wagon route extended from Independence to the present site of Portland.

During the eight years following Wyeth's first colonization venture, most of the emigration to Oregon was by New England Protestants. Then, in the spring of 1840, the Jesuit Order sent the first Catholic missionary into the Rockies. He was Father Pierre Jean De Smet, short, fat, jovial, and fearless, with deep devotion to his calling and a marvelous sense of humor. Father De Smet, a Belgian, had for ten years been a frontier missionary among the Potawatami Indians at the present site of Council Bluffs, Iowa. In April, 1840, he accompanied Andrew Drips's supply caravan from Westport Landing, now Kansas City, to the last rendezvous held by the beaver trappers.

Roly-poly Father De Smet became not only admired but beloved by the mountain men before the rendezvous ended, but he, like Father Garcés, preferred to travel alone among the Indians. From the rendezvous he struck off with a band of Flathead Indians to the general vicinity of Missoula, Montana. He visited any Indian encampments found along the way, making friends and acquainting the natives with the Cross and the story of Christ. Late that fall he crossed unharmed through the dangerous Blackfoot country, and canoed down the Missouri to Council Bluffs.

In the spring of 1841, Father De Smet returned to the Rockies, talking with him the personnel for establishing the first Catholic missions in the northern Rockies: two priests, three lay brothers, a carpenter, a blacksmith, and a tinner. Traveling in carts pulled by two mules harnessed in tandem, they accompanied Tom Fitzpatrick's trapping party to the Bear River. After crossing South Pass, Fitzpatrick led them across the valley of the Green River by the houte which would soon become famous as the Sublette Cutoff on the Oregon Trail. The route followed Pacific Creek down to the Big Sandy, then turned almost straight west, across nearly forty miles of waterless, sagebrush-covered desert to the Green. From there, it continued slightly southwest for thirty more waterless miles to Ham's Fork, and reached Bear River near the point where Wyoming, Utah, and Idaho join. Although rough on draft animals, it had advantages over the route by way of Fort Bridger, saving nearly seventy miles of travel and five creek fordings. It was taken by more than half the emigrant trains during the years that followed, the dry stretches usually being traveled at night.

Leaving Fitzpatrick at Bear River, Father De Smet and his party continued on, reaching Fort Vancouver June 8, 1842. There he found two other priests, brought across Canada by the Hudson's Bay Company. Their missions were thriving, so Father De Smet turned back to the mountains of northern Idaho and his beloved Flatheads. But his reports, letters, and journals stimulated a westward Catholic migration.

THE PATHFINDER

By the end of 1841, migration to Oregon had been considerable, but not enough to suit Senator Thomas Hart Benton of Missouri. He believed that many people had been frightened away by wildly exaggerated newspaper reports of danger from Indian attack. In casting about for a means of counteracting this unfavorable publicity, the Senator hit upon a brilliant scheme. His daughter had recently married a young second lieutenant in the Topographical Corps, John C. Frémont, who had ambitious to become a famous military leader and explorer, but whose greatest talent was for inspirational writing. As a stunt to demonstrate the absolute safety of the Oregon Trail, Benton conceived the idea of sending his twelve-year-old son as far as the Continental Divide, with Frémont to write the publicity. To carry out his scheme at Government expense, he pushed through Congress an appropriation for "mapping the Oregon Trail to the western boundary of the United States," then had Frémont assigned to the task.

There was, of course, little reason for mapping the Oregon Trail, since there were no turnoffs and a blind man could have followed the deep wagon ruts. But Frémont arrived at St. Louis in the spring of 1842 with a German topographer and enough scientific and navigational instruments for an exploration of the North Pole. In addition, he brought a large inflatable India-rubber boat for proving the navigability of the Platte and Sweetwater rivers, and a lavish array of camping equipment. At St. Louis he bought specially constructed carts and wagons, packsaddles, and nearly a hundred horses, and employed twenty-one French-Canadian voyageurs. To add glamour to the expedition, he engaged two of the most famous mountain men—Lucien Maxwell as hunter, and Kit Carson as guide.

Because of his overelaborate preparations, it was mid-June before Frémont set out from Westport Landing with his impressive cavalcade. The trek to Fort Laramie would have been routine if Frémont had not tried to be a great explorer and prove the Platte River navigable. Days were lost while he made aimless side excursions in an effort to pioneer a shorter and better route. Others were wasted in trying to use the rubber boat as a ferry, and in dragging it over sand bars in the foot-deep Platte.

When the expedition reached Fort Laramie, Carson learned that there had been a battle the previous fall between a band of Sioux and a party of sixty American traders who had plied them with frontier whiskey and tried to rob them of their furs. Eight of the Sioux had been killed, and the tribe was reported to have gone on the warpath. Carson had no fear for himself, and little for the safety of the expedition, but, believing the danger great enough that the young son of a United States Senator should not be exposed to it, he advised Frémont to leave Randolph Benton in care of the factor until the expedition returned. Frémont insisted that the boy should remain with the expedition, that if the Sioux wanted a battle he and his voyageurs would teach them a lesson. It was Carson who did the teaching. Unable to read or write, he dictated his will to the factor. That was enough for the voyageurs. If the danger were so great that Kit Carson had made his will, they had no stomach to face it. Frémont was obliged to compromise:

the boy was left at Fort Laramie and Carson convinced the voyageurs to go on.

The march to South Pass was as uneventful as that from Westport Landing to Fort Laramie, but the homeward journey had its moments of excitement. At the confluence of the Sweetwater and Platte, Frémont decided to launch his rubber boat and float triumphantly to the Missouri. The launching proved somewhat difficult in the swift water, but the rubber craft, being empty and flexible, rode easily over submerged boulders. Frémont was sure that it would be ideal for shooting rapids, and would unquestionably solve the problem of navigating swift mountain streams. Without further experiment, he had the scientific instruments, maps, journals, arms, bedding, and a good part of the provisions loaded into the boat. Carson, Maxwell, and a few of the men were sent ahead with the horses. Frémont, the topographer, and the rest of the voyageurs would ride the river, and they would all rendezvous at Fort Laramie.

With the voyageurs singing happily, the overloaded craft sped toward Fiery Narrows like an elephant on a rampage. At the mouth of the chasm it was caught and spun in a whirlpool, flinging sextant, telescope, and baggage overboard, then leaped into the flying spray of the cascades. Where the five-hundred-foot cliffs pinched closest together, the rubber steed sunfished, bucked wildly, and capsized. Battered and half drowned, Frémont and his men managed to save themselves and scale the canyon walls, but little else was salvaged.

The rest of the homeward journey was no more eventful than the westbound trek, but Frémont's account of the expedition was an inspirational masterpiece. At Government expense, Senator Benton had hundreds of thousands of copies printed and distributed throughout the East. The result was electrifying. Readers were convinced that the Oregon Trail was as safe and comfortable to travel as the streets of their own home towns; caravans were organized by the hundreds, and the great migration rolled westward from the Missouri with the greening of the grass in the spring of 1843.

The California Trail

JUST AS the Snake River determined the course of the Oregon Trail across Idaho, the Humboldt River determined the course of the California Trail across Nevada. The headwaters of the Humboldt, rising in the northeast corner of Nevada, were discovered by Peter Skene Ogden of the Hudson's Bay Company in 1828. Following the rendezvous of 1833, Captain Bonneville sent forty trappers, led by Joseph Walker, to hunt out new beaver streams west of Great Salt Lake. Joe Walker, like Frémont only in this one respect, had ambitions to be an explorer. He not only knew of Jed Smith's fame as the discoverer of an overland route to California, but of Ewing Young's success in trapping beaver there. Walker, no doubt, had his destination well in mind when he led his band westward from the rendezvous. He skirted the northern end of Great Salt Lake, then continued almost due westward for more than a hundred miles to Mary's River, the most northerly tributary of the Humboldt.

Although beaver were plentiful along the Mary's, Walker did not stop to trap, but hurried downstream, reached the Humboldt just west of present Wells, Nevada, and continued on to the southwest. For a hundred miles the river was clear and cold, with excellent beaver streams flowing in from isolated mountain ranges on either side. Then the lush grass that bordered the headwaters gave way to greasewood brush.

There were no tributaries, the water became progressively brackish, and beaver scarce. Walker would certainly have turned back if his purpose had been to discover beaver streams, but he continued on.

Each day the desert became more arid, the water more brackish, the forage scarcer, the heat more intolerable, and the horses more emaciated. Naked Digger Indians skulked through the greasewood, pouncing like a pack of snarling jackals upon any horse that lagged behind or strayed, stripping hide and flesh from its bones with their teeth. As, day after day, the animals weakened, the Diggers grew more bold, and the pack increased until they outnumbered the trappers. Doubtlessly worried, and with his patience tried, Walker ordered his men to fire upon the defenseless Indians. In the massacre a score or more, including women and children, were killed, and the everlasting enmity of the Diggers aroused. Within the next thirty years, the Indians of the Nevada deserts would repay that treachery with far more than tenfold interest.

For a hundred miles, Walker followed the Humboldt southward, his men shooting at any Indian that was seen. With each mile the river slowed and dwindled from evaporation, until it became too bitter for either man or animal to drink. Then it spread into a shallow, alkaline lake and sank into the desert. By holding straight on to the south, Walker failed to discover Truckee River, which would have led him to the best pass across the central Sierra Nevada, later to become famous as Donner Pass.

Having only a vague idea of his whereabouts, Walker continued southward, for some strange reason crossed the stream that would be known as Carson River, and reacherd the northern loop of Walker River, forty miles east of present Carson City. With the solid rampart of the Sierra Nevada in view, Walker turned up the stream to the southwest, and followed it high into the moun-

tains. Not knowing that he was retracing the general
course pioneered by Jed Smith when returning from
California in 1827, Walker crossed the summit of the
Sierras, probably by way of Sonora Pass, and descended
the Stanislaus River to the San Joaquin Valley. The
party made its way to San Francisco Bay, and turned
southward along the coast to Monterey, where it spent
the winter of 1833-34. Walker's welcome by the Spanish officials was no more cordial than Smith's had been.
In February he returned to the San Joaquin Valley, and
followed it southward to the present site of Bakersfield.
Doubtlessly knowing of Smith's arrest at Mission San
Gabriel, and wishing to avoid the risk, Walker turned
eastward, climbed the Sierra Nevada through rugged
Kern River Canyon, and crossed the summit at Walker
Pass. Skirting the foothills northward, he picked up his
trail of the previous fall and returned to the rendezvous
of 1834 by the route over which he had come.

In the fall of 1834, Kit Carson blazed the route
which would connect the Humboldt with the Overland
Trail. From Fort Hall he led his trapping band sixty
miles down Snake River, then turned southward along
Raft River to its headwaters, and westward to the
point where Idaho, Utah, and Nevada now join. There
he trapped the headwaters of Goose Creek and moved
on to the southwest, trapping Thousand Springs Creek
which flows down from three low mountain ranges and
is swallowed by the desert lying between them. A desert-
crossing of less than ten miles led to the source of
Bishop's Creek, the most easterly tributary of the
Humboldt. Carson and his men found beaver plentiful
in the nine clear streams that flow into the Humboldt
in northeastern Nevada, and moved on in search of
more. They followed the river nearly to the sink,
then turned back because there was no grazing for
the pack horses, no beaver in the brackish stream,
and provisions were running low. Thereafter the mountain men trapped the headwaters of the Humboldt each

season, following Carson's route from the Snake, but few parties went farther downstream than the present site of Battle Mountain, Nevada.

THE CALIFORNIA IMMIGRANTS

The first emigrants to pass over the California Trail were the Bidwell party. Twenty-five-year-old John Bidwell—handsome, intelligent, and imbued with the pioneer spirit—had come west in the fall of 1839 to teach school at Weston, Missouri. Soon after, he heard of the wonders of California through a letter from John Marsh, an early settler who had sailed around Cape Horn. The letter fired Bidwell's already smoldering enthusiasm, which proved so contagious that during the winter of 1840-41, he was successful in convincing five hundred Missourians to join his Western Emigration Society. In the early spring of 1841 they were to meet at Sapling Grove, each family with its own wagon, provisions, and camping equipment.

All went well until Thomas Farnham returned from leading a small party to Oregon. His reports of the hardships encountered on the overland journey were enough to discourage most of the Missourians. When Bidwell reached Sapling Grove he found only sixty-nine men, women, and children. Worse still, those who had arrived were poverty stricken, and most of them undecided as to whether they wanted to go to California or Oregon. There was less than a hundred dollars cash among the whole sixty-nine. Some were driving ox-drawn wagons, a few had come in carriages, others on horseback, and several were afoot. Knowing only that the starting point of the trail was at Independence, and that California and Oregon lay beyond the Rocky Mountains, the forlorn little party set out, and was fortunate enough to fall in with a band of mountain men led by Tom Fitzpatrick.

As with almost every emigrant organization that was to follow, discord and wrangling broke out in the Bidwell party soon after taking the trail. By the time it arrived at South Pass the party was divided into two feuding factions, one determined to go to Oregon and the other to California. At the northern bend of Bear River the feud reached a point where the two factions would no longer travel together, so Bidwell, with a group of thirty-two men, one woman, and one child decided to strike off for California. The only direction Fitzpatrick could give them was to follow the Bear to Great Salt Lake, skirt its northern end, and continue westward to pick up Carson's old trail to the Humboldt.

John Bidwell and his party followed Bear River to within ten miles of Great Salt Lake, but no one knows the exact route taken as they groped their way westward across the deserts and mountains. They were obliged to abandon their wagons, failed to find the trail, and did not discover the headwaters of the Humboldt until late September. With incredible suffering they made their way downstream to the sink, subsisting on the flesh of horses that gave out from starvation and exhaustion. Although there was no trail, they continued southward along the course Walker had taken, and reached the river that bears his name. As he had done, they followed the western branch of the river to its source, crossed the summit of the Sierra Nevada, and descended the Stanislaus River to the San Joaquin Valley. Considering that they had no knowledge of the geography of the West, no one to guide them, and no frontier experience, their achievement is one of the most amazing in American history.

With Frémont's report of his junket to South Pass having spurred the Oregon migration, Senator Benton pushed through Congress an appropriation for a second expedition. Its declared purpose was for the discovery of a more direct route to Oregon, but that was simply a subterfuge. The Senator's actual purpose was fourfold: to spy out the military strength of the British in Oregon and the Mexicans in California, and at the same time discover a direct route through the Rocky Mountains by which a migration of American citizens to California could be stimulated. In the early spring of 1843 Frémont was again in St. Louis outfitting an expedition, but this time he had conquest in mind more than exploration. He enlisted thirty-nine experienced fighting men, mulcted Colonel Kearny out of a mounted cannon from the U.S. arsenal, "for protection against the audacious Indian tribes," and sent for Carson to bring his Carson Men and guide him through the Rockies.

Carson met Frémont in Colorado during May, and told him there was no direct route by which wagons could be taken through the central Rockies, but the Pathfinder was determined to prove him wrong. He spent so many weeks blundering into blind canyons and exploring already well-known Great Salt Lake that winter caught him at Fort Hall. Carson advised him to winter there or abandon the cannon, but Frémont would do neither. He had planned to impress the British at Fort Vancouver and the Mexicans at Monterey, and would not be turned from his purpose. To drag the cannon to the Columbia River Valley through deep snow killed dozens of mules, consumed all the provisions, and exhausted the men. Half-starved, ragged, and nearly frozen, they finally reached The Dalles. Frémont left Carson there with the expedition while he went down the Columbia by boat to reconnoiter Fort Vancouver. He returned with a few sacks of beans —and the opinion that one mounted cannon would impress the Mexicans much more than the British. Hiring two Indian guides, he set off for California.

The Indians guided Frémont southward along the Deschutes River and into the Klamath marshes of southern Oregon. There they became completely lost and abandoned the party. For days the men wallowed through the marshes, dragging the anchorlike cannon, while Frémont took celestial observations and plotted a direct course to Sutter's Fort. But the direct course led to Klamath Lake, and the Cascade Range blocked a passage around it to the west. An almost direct route, now followed by U.S. Highway 97, would have led around Mount Shasta to the Sacramento Valley, but Frémont, like Jed Smith, had seen maps showing the Buena Ventura River. He decided to stay on the eastern side of the mountains until he reached the Buena Ventura, then cross to California through its canyon.

In mid-January the expedition reached the Truckee River, east of present Reno, Nevada, but Frémont, still expecting to find the Buena Ventura, would not turn up the stream. By taking celestial observations he knew Sutter's Fort to be only a hundred miles away, almost straight westward, so two weeks were lost in searching for the Buena Ventura canyon. When, at the end of January, Carson discovered the river that bears his name, the situation had become desperate. The expedition was entirely out of provisions, so could neither go into winter quarters nor turn back, and hope of finding the mythical river had to be given up. On February 6 Kit discovered nine-thousand-foot-high Carson Pass, but the snow at the summit was nearly twenty feet deep, and the noon temperature below zero. The cannon and all packs had to be abandoned, and horses—solely for food—could be gotten across the mountains only by beating out a trail with wooden mauls. The crossing required a full month, and before the exhausted expedition reached Sutter's Fort two men had gone insane from hardship, frostbite, and starvation.

Frémont was in poor condition to impress anyone. Without Carson, he would have lost his own life and the lives of his men. He had found no new route through the Rockies and had not shortened the Oregon Trail by a single inch. Still, his report of the expedition was exciting and convincing. It inspired many an emigrant to pack his family and belongings into a covered wagon and head for California.

There are various claims as to who took the first wagons overland to California, but there can be little doubt that it was Joe Walker, although the area to which he took them was not then considered to be California. In the summer of 1843 Walker led the Chiles party, traveling with three mule-drawn wagons in addition to pack horses and saddle mounts, from Fort Hall to California. From the Snake he followed the well-known trappers' trails to the Humboldt, then continued over the route by which he had returned in the spring of 1834. In the Owens Valley, now a part of eastern California, he was obliged to abandon the wagons, and crossed the Sierra Nevada with pack animals.

The first wagons were probably taken across the Sierra Nevada by the Stevens party of 1843. This expedition is of great importance to trail history, for it definitely pioneered and opened the most difficult stretch of the California Trail. In many ways the group—composed of twenty-six men, eight women, and seventeen children—was better suited to such an adventure than any other early emigrant party. It was predominantly Irish and five, or possibly six, of the wagons belonged to an intermarried family group—the Murphys, Martins, and Millers. One of the other wagons was that of "Old Man" Hitchcock, a mountain man returning to the West with his widowed daughter and her four children. Another was that of Dr. Townsend, traveling with his wife and her seventeen-year-old brother, Moses Schallenberger—the chronicler of the expedition. Of the three remaining wagons, one belonged to Allen Montgomery and his wife; one to John Sullivan, traveling with his sister and two young brothers, and the other to Elisha Stevens. Caleb Greenwood, an oldtime beaver trapper accompanied by two half-breed sons, was taken along as guide and Indian interpreter. The rest of the party was made up of unattached young men, well mounted and probably leading pack animals.

Although the Murphy contingent certainly controlled the vote, unattached Elisha Stevens was elected captain. A slight, wiry man of about forty, he had earlier been connected with the fur trade of the Northwest and, though unfamiliar with the Oregon Trail, was a thorough frontiersman. He was cautious without being timid, a strict disciplinarian without being overbearing, and sufficiently foresighted to avoid trouble before it arose.

With all the wagons ox-drawn and a few milch cows trailing behind, the caravan set out from the west bank of the Missouri, opposite Council Bluff, on May 18, 1843. Under Elisha Stevens's firm but gentle leadership there was no discord or dissension in the party, and with the exception of normal hardships on such a journey, the long trek to Fort Hall was relatively uneventful.

The caravan reached Fort Hall on August 10, and stopped for several days to rest and graze the animals, then moved on down the Snake, and two days later turned southward up Raft River Valley. In his memoirs, Schallenberger made no reference to the wheel tracks of Walker's wagons which were, no doubt, still visible, and which the party must have been following, since Greenwood knew nothing of the route beyond Snake River. In any event, the Stevens party traveled by the same general route that Walker had taken to Humboldt Sink, arriving there at the end of September. The summer of 1843 on the Nevada deserts must have been less dry than usual, for Schallenberger wrote that the grazing was good for the entire distance, and that the water, though brackish, was drinkable even at the sink.

It is not at all probable that the Stevens party followed Walker's exact trail all the way, since the deserts along a considerable part of the Humboldt are wide and greasewood-covered, making wheel tracks exceedingly easy to lose. It is even less probable that they discovered his trail leading southward from the sink. Otherwise, Stevens would doubtlessly have continued on the same course, rather than stopping a week to search out the way to California. The party was still undecided when a band of Paiute Indians came to the sink, among them their aged chief, whose name Greenwood understood to be Truckee. Actually, what he took to be the name was a Paiute word of agreement, meaning *all right* or *very well*. The chief—father of Winnemucca, who would be the scourge of white men in the Nevada deserts for more than twenty years—was affable, highly intelligent, and thoroughly acquainted with the deserts and mountains. He understood Greenwood's sign language perfectly, knew where Sutter's Fort was, and the best way to get there. Squatting, he drew a map on the ground. Two suns to the west there was a river flowing eastward from a great canyon in the mountains, and beyond the head of the canyon the streams flowed down to the white man's fort. Halfway to the river, water would be found at hot springs.

The start was made early on the morning of October 8, following the general route that is now Highway 40. The hot springs were not reached until midnight. Water was cooled in tubs for the suffering animals, but few would drink, and those that did sickened. Stevens ordered the caravan on through the night, and at two o'clock the next afternoon it reached the river, thirty-five miles east of present Reno. With no food, water, or rest in thirty-two hours, the animals were at the point of exhaustion. Although the emigrants had suffered far less than their stock, the desert crossing must have seemed interminable to them, for Moses Schallenberger estimated the distance to be eighty miles. It was actually only forty, and this stretch of the trail is still known as Forty-Mile Desert.

Even though Stevens was anxious to push on, so as

to cross the Sierra Nevada before winter set in, he stopped two days to let the animals graze and recuperate from the ordeal of the dry crossing. Unlike many captains who were to follow his trail during the next ten years, he gave as much attention to the welfare of the animals in his charge as to the humans. By doing so, he had brought the oxen through in better shape than when they left Missouri. Their bodies were lean and tough, and their unshod hoofs had become as hard as polished ebony.

Probably on the morning of October 12, the Stevens party started westward along the river they had named for old Truckee. Highway 40 now follows the general course of the river, the distance to the town of Truckee is less than seventy miles, and if it were not for passing through Sparks and Reno a tourist would easily make the drive in an hour and a half. It is true that the first thirty miles of roadway, along the hillsides of the lower canyon through the Virginia Mountains, is somewhat winding. But the run across Truckee Meadows, with Reno at the center, is almost level. West of the meadows the road enters the throat of the upper canyon, which narrows as it penetrates deeper into the Sierra. The hills become steeper, the roadway a bit shaky, and in places the cautious driver might slow down to forty miles an hour. If he is careless enough to enjoy the scenery as he drives, he may catch a glimpse of the clear mountain stream, brawling around great boulders as it winds and twists through the canyon below. But Highway 40 was not there in 1843, and no white man had ever followed the twisting, brawling Truckee.

In the lower canyon the Stevens party was often unable to travel more than two or three miles in a day. On precipitous hillsides the wagons had to be unloaded, and held with guy ropes to keep them from tipping over. To get through at all, the river often had to be crossed three or four times in a single day, and with each crossing the horn of the oxen's hoofs softened.

Back on the rocky hillsides the softened hoofs wore down rapidly and oxen went lame. Sparing them as much as possible, Elisha Stevens pushed on. October was drawing toward its end, there had already been flurries of snow, and the summit of the Sierras must be crossed before winter set in.

Above the meadows the caravan was nearly stalled. Where the river flows northward along the present California–Nevada line, the canyon walls pinched in so close that the only possible passage for wagons was in the rocky bed of the stream. Men were obliged to wade in waist-deep icy water, straining at the wheels and lifting them over boulders. The oxen's feet had become so tender that the poor beasts would not take a step without goading. To lighten the wagons, everything possible was loaded onto the saddle horses, and the women and children scrambled along the margin of the river as best they could. The only feed for the animals was a few rushes growing by the stream, and with each day the stock grew thinner and weaker. Then the sky clouded over and a foot of snow fell.

It is believed that the Stevens party reached the present site of Truckee, California, on November 14, after thirty-two days of fighting their way less than seventy miles up the river. A mile farther on, the main stream turned abruptly to the south, and a branch continued to the west. The canyon to the south was steep and rugged, while that along the branch was wide enough to permit the passage of a wagon. Here Stevens split his party. The sky had not cleared since the snowfall, and another storm appeared to be coming on. Sutter's Fort could not be far away, but if the entire party took the wrong route and were snowbound there would be no chance of turning back or sending ahead for relief. Choosing four fo the best hunters among the young men, and two of the younger women, Stevens mounted them on the strongest horses and sent them up the south canyon. They were to cross the summit, find the fort, and arrange for a rescue party if the expected storm struck.

The mounted party ascended Truckee River to the western shore of Lake Tahoe, found a pass through the high mountains, and discovered a stream flowing to the west—probably the Middle Fork of the American River. Living entirely upon game, fording the ice-cold stream time and again, and often forced to find a way around impassable gorges, they reached Sutter's Fort on December 10.

When the party was split, the wagon division followed the western branch of the Truckee two miles and a half. There they found a large lake, but beyond its farther end the canyon was blocked solidly by high mountains. Stevens moved the wagons along the north side of the lake for a short distance, then made camp where wood was plentiful and there was a little grazing for the cattle. Two days were spent in searching for a pass across the summit. A spot very close to that at which Highway 40 now crosses was finally chosen, but the oxen were too exhausted to pull loaded wagons up the steep mountainside. It was decided to abandon all but five wagons, and for the men to back-pack necessary bedding and the remaining provisions to the top of the pass.

Above the canyon floor the snow was two or more feet deep, and in places the mountain was so steep that an empty wagon could hardly be taken up. At one ledge near the summit the oxen had to be led up through a narrow defile, then a wagon dragged to the top with half a dozen yokes straining at chains while men hoisted from below. Five days of back-breaking labor were required to drag the wagons to the top of the 7189-foot pass, then Dr. Townsend became worried. He had invested most of his savings in broadcloth, silk, and other light fabrics which would bring high prices in California. If left in his abandoned wagon until spring, the goods would certainly be stolen by Indians, and he would be financially ruined.

Moses Schallenberger, Dr. Townsend's brother-in-law, offered to stay behind and guard the wagons until a relief party could be sent back from Sutter's Fort. He was an excellent hunter and was sure he would have no trouble in shooting plenty of game. Two other men, Foster and Montgomery, offered to stay with him. It was generally agreed that they would be safe enough, but Stevens insisted that two cows, too thin and footsore for hard travel, be left with them. They would supply a little milk, and could be butchered in the event of poor hunting. With the young men provided for, the wagon party moved westward from the summit. For three days they made their way along the route that is now Highway 40. Some twenty miles beyond the pass they were caught in a raging snowstorm. When the storm subsided, the seventeen younger men set out to find Sutter's Fort, leaving the two eldest with the women and children. They reached the fort on December 13, just as a rescue party was starting out, and those left at the wagons were soon brought in.

Back in the canyon Schellenberger and his two companions had barely time to build themselves a shack before they were caught in the same storm that marooned the wagon party. Snow piled three or four feet deep, the cows could find no feed, and no game could be hunted. For a few days the men made out with what few scraps of food had been left in the wagons, then butchered the starving cows, as much to put them out of their suffering as for meat. But there was little meat on the cows, half-starved for more than a month, and no game was astir in the deep snow.

One snowstorm followed another, no hunting could be done, and by mid-December only one thin quarter of beef remained. Unless help arrived before it was gone, or unless the men could get out on snowshoes, it seemed certain that they would die of starvation.

None of them was experienced with snowshoes, but Foster and Montgomery fashioned three pairs from ox-bows and rawhide, while Schallenberger stripped and dried the meat. In their ignorance they bound the snow-shoes to their feet at both toe and heel, and set out for the pass. At each step the clumsy shoes sank deep into the loose snow. Being secured at the heel, they had to be raised straight up, lifting snow as if they were shovels. Before the top of the pass was reached, Schallenberger became exhausted and was nearly crippled with leg cramps. The mature men could go on, but he could not. They had no choice but to give him the largest share of the dried meat and let him go back to the shack, hoping that a rescue party could get through before he starved to death. But Moses Schallenberger was too ingenious to starve. There were traps in one of the wagons, and fox and coyote tracks in the snow. Until he was rescued on February 26, 1844, he kept in good health on roasted foxes, but coyote meat was too strong to be stomached, even on the days when he had to go hungry.

Three years later the Donner party encountered exactly the same situation at the same place, but with far different results. The Donner tragedy, the most famous in American trail history, was brought about largely by the chicanery of Lansford Hastings. Ambitious, dishonest, and a clever propagandist, Hastings had arrived in California by sea in 1843, when the first surge of Oregon migration was at its crest. He was quick in observing the weakness of the Mexican Government, and equally quick in devising a scheme for turning it to his own advantage. Thousands of American immigrants were pouring into Oregon, but only a few trickling into California. If he could divert the tide he believed he could overthrow the Mexicans, set up an independent nation, and establish himself as ruler. In an effort to do so he published and distributed throughout the East his *Emigrants' Guide to Oregon and Cal-*

ifornia, extolling the glories of California and damning Oregon with faint praise. With practically no knowledge of the geography, and no investigation, he invented the Hastings Cutoff, and assured prospective emigrants that by taking it they could reach California quickly and easily. They would simply turn their wagons away from the Oregon Trail at Bridger's Fort, "bearing west southwest, to the Salt Lake; and thence continue down to the Bay of San Francisco."

The Donner brothers, well-to-do Illinois farmers in their early sixties, were among the thousands who became enthralled by Hastings's propaganda. They sold their farms, loaded the families and household furniture into specially built wagons, and set out for California in April, 1846. The spring travel over the trail was heavy, one caravan following another across the Kansas prairies. But no group stayed intact long after the outset. Wrangling broke out under the monotony of the plodding pace, and the most restless pulled out to join faster moving caravans. The Donners were in no hurry. They accepted Hastings's assurances as they accepted the Scripture—on faith and without rationalization—and were confident that by the cutoff route they could easily reach San Francisco Bay in early fall. In spite of warnings by oldtime frontiersmen that the cutoff was impractical and dangerous, they dropped back, letting the unbelievers surge ahead. Gradually they were joined by other Hastings converts.

Leisurely following at the trail end of the spring migration, the heterogeneous group of eighty-seven men, women, and children—leaderless, and united only by their unquestioning faith in Hastings's propaganda— arrived at Bridger's Fort on July 28. Still in no hurry, the Donner party rested until August 1, then set out to the southwest on an old trappers' trail leading into the Wasatch Mountains. The going was rough, but eight or ten miles a day were traveled until the caravan reached the Weber River, where the trail entered a narrow canyon, impassable to wagons. It was too late to turn back and take the established route, or winter would surely catch them before they could cross the Sierra Nevada. Baffled, and with their faith in Hastings completely shattered, the party began to panic. Blaming each other for their predicament, the men seized axes and crowbars, and frantically started hacking a roadway around the canyon. Gentle and kindly George Donner did his best to keep peace, but he was not a strong leader. Each day the panic increased and the discord erupted into feuds. Bickering and quarreling, the party fought its way through the Wasatch Mountains for more than a month, and reached Salt Lake in mid-September, completely disorganized.

Miraculously, only one human life was lost in crossing the Nevada deserts, but many of the wagons had to be abandoned, provisions ran low, and more than half the livestock was lost to drought, starvation, and Indian arrows. Still quarreling and disorganized, the Donner party reached the foot of the pass which would thereafter bear their name on the afternoon of November 3. It had begun to snow, but the men were tired, so decided to pitch camp and make the crossing next morning. By evening a howling blizzard was raging. It lasted several days, piling three feet of snow in the canyon, and when it ended the party discovered that its cattle had drifted away.

Only forty-seven of the Donner party survived, and the gruesome story of its resorting to cannibalism is too well-known to need repeating. Victims of chicanery, gullibility, panic, and weak leadership, they suffered an ordeal that is almost beyond belief, but news of their tragedy doubtlessly saved the lives of many who might have followed in their footsteps. By the time the last members of the party were rescued the American flag was flying over California, and within six months a stream of immigrants was pouring through the gateway known as Donner Pass.

THE MORMON MIGRATION

In April, 1847, Brigham Young led the first migration of Mormons westward from Winter Quarters, near Omaha, Nebraska. These people were seeking a Promised Land, but were not deluded into believing they might find a second Garden of Eden. Young had already had the land spied out, and chosen a narrow strip between Great Salt Lake and the Wasatch Mountains, a region so arid that Jim Bridger offered to pay a thousand dollars for the first bushel of corn raised on it. Young's purpose was to carve out of the wilderness a refuge for his people, so far from civilization that they would be safe from such persecution as they had suffered in Missouri and Illinois, and where they might prosper through hard work, industry, and frugality.

The preceding fall fifteen thousand Mormons had gathered at Winter Quarters, but a mass migration was impossible, since they had been stripped of all their property and most of their livestock when driven out of Illinois. The entire sect was destitute of funds, and there were neither wagons nor draft animals enough to transport half the people. The only hope was to send work battalions ahead to establish a foothold, while the rest remained to raise crops. Then groups would migrate as best they could when a place had been provided for them in the new Zion.

It was the advance battalion of 143 carefully selected men between the ages of thirty and fifty that Young led westward. The caravan, drawn by oxen, mules, and horses, consisted of seventy-three wagons and a leather ferryboat that was mounted on wheels. In addition, nineteen milch cows were taken along, and a crate of poultry hung from the tailboard of nearly every wagon.

Sad experience had taught the Mormons to stay clear of "Gentiles" as much as possible. To avoid the throng of emigrants on the Oregon Trail, Young led his caravan up the Platte Valley on the north side of the river, but the Mormons traveled in an entirely different manner from any others who had pioneered a new trail. Hard work was a part of their creed, and Young enforced it rigidly. Furthermore, he was preparing a way for his people who were to follow. He kept a road-building crew well out in front, cutting down gulch banks, bridging creeks where timber was available, and preparing camp sites. When buffalo country was reached, he set his men to jerking meat for the next winter, but allowed no more animals to be killed than necessary.

By traveling from dawn till dusk, the Mormon caravan outdistanced the spring migration before reaching Fort Laramie. A short distance below the fort it crossed to the south side of the river and continued along the established trail. At the regular crossing, near where Casper, Wyoming, now stands, the river was in flood. After swimming the livestock across, the wagons were ferried easily in the leather boat, bringing an idea into Brigham Young's ingenious mind: A horde of Gentiles was swarming up the trail, eager to reach California or Oregon as soon as possible. Rather than lose time in cutting logs and building rafts, many of them would pay fifty pounds of flour to have a wagon ferried across. He christened the boat *Revenue Cutter,* and left a dozen men to operate it. Until the spring rush had passed they were busy night and day, and the revenue they collected went far toward feeding the Mormon pioneers until a crop could be raised in the new land.

The Mormons were first after the Donner party to take the cutoff route from Fort Bridger, but their experiences were quite different. Beyond the Weber River Canyon they found that the panicked Donner party had hacked its way blindly. Camp was pitched, and a thorough survey of the mountains made, in which the route that is now Highway 30S was discovered. The entire battalion set to work, and within less than a week had opened a clear passage to Salt Lake. On July 24 Brigham Young, desperately ill with mountain fever, was carried to the mouth of a canyon above present Salt Lake City. He scanned the arid land that sloped away toward the distant lake, cut off from the Great Plains by five hundred miles of rugged mountains, and from California by an equally wide barrier of burning deserts, then spoke his famous words, "This is the place."

By late August fifty acres had been plowed, irrigation canals were being dug to bring water from the mountains, a plot the size of a city block had been surrounded by a stout log stockade, and half a dozen cabins built. Under irrigation the land had proved fertile, so Young hurried messengers back to Winter Quarters. A work force of fifteen hundred young men and women were to take the trail the following spring, bringing all the wagons, livestock, household furniture, seed, and farming equipment that could be spared.

The caravan of 1848 was made up of five hundred and sixty wagons, leaving the Saints at Winter Quarters almost destitute of transport, but ingenious Brigham Young met the situation by having his people build themselves handcarts. During the next four years more than three thousand of these carts were pulled over the one-thousand-and-thirty-mile trail to Salt Lake City. With a man in the shafts, and women or children pushing from behind, a five-hundred-pound load could be carried, and thirty miles were often traveled in a day— more than double the average distance of a wagon train. One party dragged its carts fourteen hundred miles from Iowa City to Salt Lake in nine weeks, and suffered fewer deaths than most of the Gentiles' wagon parties. All the Saints were not so fortunate. In one company a sixth of the members died of starvation and frostbite, but the migration went on without a halt. By 1849 Salt Lake City had become a thriving community of five thousand inhabitants, surrounded by hundreds of fertile farms. Although there were two Mormons with James Marshall when he discovered gold at Sutter's Mill, Brigham Young would not permit his people to take any part in the California gold rush. Still, it was a godsend to them.

In the spring of 1849 the Overland Trail was so thronged with gold rushers that there was seldom a time when one party was not within sight of another. Anxious to be first in reaching the gold fields, many of these early Argonauts were too impatient to take the long California Trail by way of Fort Hall and Raft River, so followed the Mormon roadway from Bridger's Fort to Salt Lake City. To supplement their provisions before crossing the deserts, they would have paid high prices for any farm produce the Mormons could spare, but Young would not let his people traffic with them. Contact with the Gentiles had always led to resentment and persecution. He had brought the Saints into the wilderness to avoid it, and had no intention of letting the bars down. Most feared of all were the Missourians, but there were two among them who were trusted and admired. They were Colonel Alexander Doniphan and Ben Holladay. Doniphan had befriended the Mormons, saving many of their lives by warning them of impending attacks when they were driven out of Missouri, and Holladay had been his personal courier.

THE FREIGHTERS AND THE MAIL SUBSIDY

From early youth, Ben Holladay had been an astute, farsighted businessman. During the Mexican War he had made and saved several thousand dollars, operating sutler wagons with the Army of the West. At the close of the war he opened a trading post at Weston, Missouri, across the river from Fort Leavenworth, and it had prospered. Young Holladay was quick to recognize the opportunity presented by the Mormon migration and the gold rush. He reasoned that California, with its tremendous influx of population, must be badly in need of provisions. He believed the Mormons had those provisions but would not trade with the Gentiles, and that they themselves must be in need of clothing, utensils, tools, and other merchandise of civilization. Borrowing every dime he could raise, he bought fifty Conestoga wagons, loaded them with seventy thousand dollars' worth of the sort of merchandise most needed by the Mormons, and set off for Salt Lake City.

Brigham Young welcomed Holladay, not only as a trader but a friend, and accepted the entire caravan—merchandise, wagons, and draft animals—paying for it largely in cattle at six dollars a head and flour at a dollar a hundred pounds. Holladay arranged to use the wagons for three months, loaded his flour on them, and set out across the deserts and mountains for California, driving a herd of more than a thousand beef cattle. The trail across the Nevada deserts was already well marked by the skeletons of animals lost by the gold rushers. Driving so large a herd, and with little grazing for it, Holladay left many a marker along the barren trail, but his profit from the venture was fantastic. In the mining camps some of his cattle sold for as high as fifty cents a pound, and his flour for as much as twenty dollars a sack. The next year he doubled the size of his caravan, and the size of his profit. The Mormon trade remained Holladay's exclusively, but he soon had a rival for the transportation business of the rapidly expanding West.

The great overland freighting industry was born of the Army's inability to supply troops during the Mexican War. In the spring of 1848 James Brown was awarded a contract to haul a hundred tons of freight from Independence to Santa Fe at $11.75 per hundredweight. The War Department was so well pleased with his performance that he was awarded much larger contracts in 1849 and 1850. To finance the venture he formed a partnership with William Russell, a financier, promoter, and politician. Brown died soon after, and Russell organized the firm of Russell, Majors & Waddell. With headquarters at Leavenworth, the firm dominated the overland transportation business until the outbreak of the Civil War. By 1856 it had established freight stations from the Missouri River to the Pacific coast. Thereafter, there was seldom a time, except when the mountain passes were clogged with snow, that a dozen or more of its freighting caravans were not rolling along the route which had come to be known as the Central Overland Trail.

Although freighting constituted the larger part of the traffic over the central route, mail service had a far greater effect upon the development of overland transportation. It also resulted in opening a new California section of the Overland Trail. Until 1851 the only overland mail was that carried to Salt Lake City by Ben Holladay as an accommodation to the Mormons. But when California became a state its citizens demanded that the Federal Government furnish them regular overland mail service. Congress responded in a rather half-hearted manner, advertising for bids to supply monthly service. Holladay, who was already toying with the idea of establishing a stagecoach line, offered to supply mail service between the Missouri River and Salt Lake City for forty-five thousand dollars per year, but the contract was awarded to Samuel Woodson at about half the figure. At the same time George Chorpenning was awarded a contract to carry the mail between Salt Lake City and San Francisco at fourteen thousand dollars per year.

Soon after the beginning of the gold rush the round-about Raft River section of the original California Trail was abandoned. In spite of the eighty-mile waterless trek across the Great Salt Lake Desert, the anxious Argonauts took the Mormon road from Fort Bridger to Salt Lake City, then followed the route which is now Highway 40 to intersect the original trail at Wells,

Nevada. To avoid the blistering salt flats and shorten the distance to San Francisco, Chorpenning pioneered a new course for his mail route. It led south along the Jordan River to Utah Lake, skirted the southern end of Great Salt Lake Desert, and struck westward to the present location of Austin, Nevada. From there to Sacramento his course was roughly that now followed by Highway 50. Chorpenning's route soon became the mainline for overland freighters, and later for stagecoach lines and the Pony Express.

Both Woodson and Chorpenning expected to make excellent profits on their contracts by hauling light freight and express along with the mail sacks, but soon found that the subsidies were far too small to cover the expenses of monthly service. They struggled along through the summer and fall of 1851, but when winter snows filled the mountain passes the service collapsed. Mail piled high on both sides of the Rockies and Sierra Nevada, and the Californians' demand for fast, dependable, weekly mail and passenger service became too vehement to be ignored by Congress. It advertised for new bids, the mail to be carried on fast passenger coaches. Ben Holladay submitted offers on both the eastern and western divisions, but was outbid on the former. He was awarded the contract between Salt Lake City and Sacramento at fifty thousand dollars per year, and invested an enormous sum in building relay stations and equipping the line, but it was a dismal failure. Great as the clamor for rapid transportation had been, there were few passengers, and the cost of manning and operating the line was tremendous. Although he had for several years been ambitious to establish a transcontinental stagecoach line, it soon became clear to him that such a venture could be successful only with a Government subsidy of at least a half-million dollars. Unlike most men who have made a bad investment, Holladay swallowed his loss and got out at the end of his first year.

For several years the California mail service was operated on a hit-or-miss basis, with subsidies increased each time a contractor went bankrupt. By 1856 John Hockaday was being paid one hundred and ninety thousand dollars annually for carrying the mail from the Missouri River to Salt Lake City, and Chorpenning was receiving one hundred and thirty thousand dollars for carrying it over his old route to San Francisco, but the service was far from satisfactory. The mail, along with express and an occasional passenger was hauled in mule-drawn wagons. In summer it sometimes got through from the Missouri to California in as few as thirty-two days; in winter it was often as many as ninety, but still the contractors could not make expenses. Then, in 1857, Congress voted a subsidy of six hundred thousand dollars for semiweekly mail and passenger service, each trip to be made in twenty-five days or less. Both Holladay and his powerful rival, Russell, Majors & Waddell, entered bids for service by way of the Central Overland route, but the contract was awarded to Butterfield & Company.

When it was discovered that the Butterfield route lay entirely through the South, the North sent up a howl of protest, demanding that Congress also establish rapid mail and passenger service by way of the much shorter Central Overland route. In a spectacular bid to outdo Butterfield, William Russell immediately made an offer for his firm to provide daily stagecoach service at an annual subsidy of nine hundred thousand dollars. A bill to authorize the subsidy was presented to Congress, but was blocked by southern Senators on grounds that the northern Rockies and Sierra Nevada were impassable in winter.

Soon after the bill was blocked, gold was discovered in Colorado. Russell believed that Denver would boom as San Francisco had, and that a stagecoach line connecting it with the Missouri River would make fabulous profits. When his partners opposed the venture he formed a separate company, borrowed heavily, and made a huge investment in coaches, horses, relay stations, and equipment. But the line suffered tremendous losses from the beginning, and soon became hopelessly insolvent. Russell was a plunger and not always ethical in his financial manipulations, but Majors and Waddell were scrupulously honest—and extremely jealous of their reputations. Fearing that Russell's failure would reflect upon the freighting firm, they agreed to let it take over the bankrupt stagecoach line and pay off the debts.

Although Russell was in close contact with Washington and must have known that it was no more than wishful thinking, he assured his partners that the nine-hundred-thousand-dollar subsidy bill would not only pass the Senate but that he could secure the contract if Hockaday and Chorpenning were bought out and fast year-round stagecoach service established on the Central Overland route. He pointed out that the firm already had numerous freight depots along the route, and large numbers of idle oxen during the winter months. The depots would serve as relay stations, considerably reducing the cost of building a stage line. The idle oxen could be used on snowplows in the Rockies and Sierra Nevada, keeping the roads open for winter travel by both stagecoaches and freight caravans, and thus increasing the freighting profits.

Deluded by Russell's assurances, his partners agreed to the plan. Hockaday and Chorpenning were bought out, scores of additional relay stations built, the facilities of the defunct stage line transferred to the Central Overland route, and semiweekly service established to Sacramento. The cost of building the line was enormous. This on top of having bailed out Russell's bankrupt business left the great firm short of funds, but astute Ben Holladay, extraordinarily wealthy from his exclusive Mormon trade, was glad to lend his giant competitor whatever money it needed. All he asked was a fair rate of interest and a chattel mortgage.

With the fresh supply of cash Russell, Majors & Waddell bought additional coaches and horses, established camps to keep the mountain roads open in winter, and cut the running time between Leavenworth and Sacramento to twenty-five days or less. Within a year its service was fully equal to Butterfield's, but still no subsidy for the central route was voted by Congress, and the cost of operation was staggering. Time and again the firm found itself pressed for funds, but Ben Holladay was always glad to make a loan—for an additional chattel mortgage.

THE PONY EXPRESS

By the close of 1859 conditions in the United States had reached so critical a stage that civil war appeared inevitable. If it should come, California's wealth might well determine the outcome, and California was very doubtful. Although admitted to the Union as a free state, it might swing to the southern cause unless kept in contact with the North by far more rapid communication than could be supplied by stagecoach mail. Whether from patriotism or in hope that it would lead to the coveted mail subsidy, William Russell stepped forward with an astounding offer: By using swift saddle horses in short relays, his firm would supply semi-weekly ten-day mail service between St. Joseph and San Francisco for five hundred dollars a round trip.

Russell's partners were appalled when he told them of his offer. The cost of building and equipping such a line might well be ruinous in their strained financial condition. Moreover, five hundred dollars a round trip would cover only a small fraction of the operating costs. But neither Majors nor Waddell felt that they could honorably repudiate the offer, even though no contract had been awarded. With another large loan from Holladay, eighty additional relay stations were built and supplied along the 1966-mile route. Four hundred of the fastest horses available were bought, and two hundred keepers and stablemen hired, together with eighty of the most courageous young frontier riders that could be found. To the booming of cannon and screaming of excited crowds, the first Pony Express riders dashed from opposite ends of the line at dusk on April 3, 1860.

Circumstances seemed to conspire against the Pony Express from the moment the first riders leaped into their saddles. The spring of 1860 was unusually cold and wet. Rain was falling in a downpour when, at 2:15 A.M. on April 4, Sam Hamilton galloped out of Sacramento with the St. Joseph mail mochila flung over his saddle. By dawn the rain had turned to snow, but Hamilton was sixty miles to the east, tossing the mochila to "Boston" Upson, high in the foothills of the Sierra Nevada. Twenty years old, five feet tall, and the son of a wealthy California newspaper publisher, Boston had roamed the Sierras from childhood, and knew them as no other white man did. His carrying of the first Pony mail over the summit is one of the most amazing feats in American frontier history.

Above the four-thousand-foot level a raging blizzard was blowing, and gales at more than sixty miles an hour piled snow fifteen to twenty feet deep. The trail was completely obliterated, and visibility reduced to less than a hundred feet, but Boston fought his way upwards from one isolated relay post afoot, shouldering the mochila and leaving his pony bogged belly deep in a snowdrift. Beyond the summit the blizzard was less severe, and at 2:18 in the afternoon he rode a staggering pony into Friday's Station on Lake Tahoe. In a storm that few men could have lived through, he had carried the first Pony mail fifty-five miles across the high hump of the Sierra Nevada in just eight hours, better time than the fastest stagecoaches could make in summer weather.

At the eastern end of the line the riders were less able to cope with the fast schedule. Rainfall was almost continuous, the Platte Valley a quagmire of deep mud, the nights dead black, and misfortune lurked in the darkness. One rider was caught in a buffalo stampede during a night thunderstorm. Another was delayed five hours while fighting off a wolf pack from a pony exhausted by the deep mud. A third rode into a relay post to find the stable empty and the keeper badly wounded by raiding Indians. With his pony already jaded, it took him half the night to reach the next post. The eastern boys fell twenty hours behind the schedule, but the desert riders more than made it up. At 3:55 on the afternoon of April 13, the first Pony Express mail reached St. Joseph. An hour and thirty-five minutes later a rider galloped his pony into Sacramento with the mochila from the East.

From the time of the Joe Walker massacre, the Paiute Indians had been the white man's unrelenting enemy. But there had been very little tribal organization, and attacks were confined to those of roving bands that skulked the trail along the Humboldt River. Then, in 1859, the richest silver deposit the world had ever known was discovered in the Washoe hills of western Nevada. These hills were covered with piñon pine, and were the winter headquarters of Chief Winnemucca and his Paiute tribesmen, who gathered from the deserts to subsist on piñon nuts. During the winter of 1859-60 a rabble of frenzied fortune seekers stampeded into the Washoes, overrunning the hills, fighting for a claim no larger than a blanket, chopping down the piñon pine, and killing any Indian who showed his head.

Although the Paiutes were the most primitive Indians on the continent, Winnemucca was an able and intelligent chief. In retaliation for the killings he organized his warriors, laid a clever ambush, and led a band of drunken prospectors into it. The cry of *massacre* was raised, the miners demanded that the Federal Government protect its citizens, and a troop of cavalry was rushed from California to annihilate the murderous Indians. But before the soldiers got across the mountains, Winnemucca and his tribesmen had disappeared into the deserts where no cavalry could follow. For more than a year they carried on so fierce a campaign that no caravan could cross the Nevada deserts without a military escort. The isolated Pony Express relay posts, strung at twenty-five to thirty mile intervals along the old Chorpenning mail route, became the chief target for raiding Paiutes. Howling like wolves, a band of a hundred or more would swoop down on a lonely post, killing keeper, hostler, and guards; pillaging, burning buildings and haystacks, and driving away the relay horses.

By the fall of 1860 more than half the Pony Express posts between Carson City and Utah Lake had been destroyed and Paiute ambushes set in every mountain pass along the trail. But except for one short period the mail went through. Never following exactly the same route twice in succession, and avoiding the regular mountain passes whenever possible, the riders made their way across the deserts as best they could, depending upon the speed of their superior mounts to outrun surprise attacks. But as more and more relay posts were destroyed the advantage of speed was lost, for a horse often had to be ridden a hundred miles to reach a remaining post. Many a rider was wounded by Indian arrows but, miraculously, only one was killed. The mail was often late, sometimes as much as a week, but no rider ever turned back, and only one refused to make his run.

That no Pony Express rider ever turned back stands as one of the finest examples of courage in American history. That Russell, Majors & Waddell never turned

back should stand equally high as an example of
patriotism. It well may be that William Russell's offer
to provide California with ten-day service at the ridic-
ulously low price of five hundred dollars a round trip
was made solely in hope it would result in his firm
being awarded the coveted contract. And it is certain
that Majors and Waddell agreed to stand by the offer
because they believed it necessary in order to uphold
the honor of the firm. But if honor was ever involved,
the firm was absolved of any obligation, either moral
or legal, before the end of 1860, since legislation
authorizing payment for the services had been blocked
by southern Senators. Although Russell, Majors &
Waddell faced almost certain ruin if the exorbitantly
expensive service were continued, its need to the Union
was becoming greater with every passing day. The firm
went deeper into debt and kept the ponies running.

By February, 1861, war appeared to be a certainty,
and California was leaning toward the Confederate
cause. Its remaining loyal to the Union depended largely
upon the policies set forth in Lincoln's inaugural address and speed in transmitting the address to Sacramento. At a cost of seventy-five thousand dollars Russell, Majors & Waddell prepared the Pony Express to
make its supreme effort. Hundreds of extra men were
hired, scores of temporary relay posts established, and
a small army of guards, keepers, and hostlers sent into
the Nevada desert. By Inauguration Day fast relay
horses were posted at ten-mile intervals along the entire
1966-mile route, and the finest riders assigned to the
most difficult sections of the trail.

"Pony Bob" Haslam was chosen for the most hazardous assignment; that of carrying the President's
address 120 miles across Paiute-infested western Nevada. Heavily armed guards were stationed at all the
relay posts, but it was impossible to give the riders
any protection on the trail, and the Paiutes were on a
rampage. Pony Bob had hoped to make his run under

cover of darkness, but the mochila containing the address reached Smith's Creek soon after dawn. Within less than two minutes Haslam was galloping away to the west. With fresh horses at Mount Airy and Castle Rock, he made the fastest time ever ridden to Cold Spring. He was at first surprised, then worried, when no Indians tried to ambush him in either of the mountain passes. To the west of Cold Spring the trail led through a wide desert valley, thickly dotted with sage brush and greasewood. Since the Paiutes had left the passes, Pony Bob reasoned that they had probably set an ambush in the valley, but circling it would cost three or four hours. Without hesitation he spurred straight down the trail, reins around the saddle horn and a pistol in each hand.

As Haslam expected, war-painted Indians boiled out of the brush like a pack of rabid wolves, and arrows filled the air like straws in a hurricane. But this was no ordinary ambush. He had no sooner broken through the main body of the pack than he was surrounded by mounted warriors, several on stolen Pony Express horses, too swift to be outrun. His only chance lay in outdistancing the others, then picking off the Express ponies one by one. Haslam won through in a running battle of more than two miles, but an arrow from close range ripped through his mouth, fracturing his jaw and knocking out five teeth. Another lodged in his left arm at the shoulder, leaving it paralyzed and useless. At the next relay station he stopped only to have the arrow cut out of his arm, and to mumble, "Fetch me a clean rag to hold in my mouth; I'm going on through."

Pony Bob Haslam did go through. When he reached Fort Churchill his face was unrecognizable, and his arm swollen larger than his thigh, but he had brought Lincoln's address one hundred and twenty miles in eight hours and two minutes, and had changed mounts twelve times. Just seven days and seventeen hours after the address was telegraphed from Washington to St.

Joseph, a Pony rider galloped it into Sacramento. No such feat of speed, endurance, and courage was ever before accomplished, but swift as the ponies had been they were not fast enough to keep up with the demands of the changing times. Their famous run was barely completed before telegraph lines were being strung from both ends of the trail. For seven months the ponies raced across the deserts and mountains, shuttling messages between the advancing lines of poles. In October, 1861, the lines met, the wires were joined, and the Pony Express had fulfilled its destiny.

6

Heyday of the Old Trails

IN ADDITION to the telegraph, it was imperative that California be bound to the Union by more rapid and frequent passenger service. A week after Lincoln's inauguration a contract with a one-million-dollar annual subsidy was authorized for daily stagecoach service over the central route, but it was too late to save Russell, Majors & Waddell. After pouring five hundred thousand dollars into the Pony Express, and losing an equal amount in operating its California stage line, the firm was too near bankruptcy to provide the necessary service. The contract was awarded to Butterfield and Company, with the proviso that its operations be transferred to the Central Overland route. A few months later the firm of Russell, Majors & Waddell was taken over by Ben Holladay, its largest creditor. Not long after, Butterfield sold out to Wells Fargo & Company.

During the Civil War freighting and stagecoaching on the Central Overland Trail reached its glorious peak. Denver, Salt Lake, and Virginia City were booming. Eastern Kansas and Nebraska were dotted with towns, and California was growing like a yearling colt. In 1863 alone, the Washoe hills poured out twenty million dollars in bullion. To haul supplies and equipment across the Sierras required two thousand men, five thousand wagons, and thirty thousand mules. From the Missouri to the Pacific a hundred or more great freight caravans were constantly on the trail and its numerous branches. Double that number of stagecoaches sped over the well-worn thoroughfare night and day. Ben Holladay had become fabulously wealthy, and the competition fierce between him and Wells Fargo. For four years the two great rivals fought each other for the transcontinental passenger business, each trying to outdo the other in speed and the magnificence of their coaches.

Wells Fargo & Company often tried to buy out Holladay, but he would never sell. Then, in October, 1866, wily Ben suddenly changed his mind and sold out to his colossal rival for more than two million dollars. He was becoming skeptical. Ever since the outbreak of the Civil War there had been plans for a transcontinental railroad, but little progress had been made beyond the surveying of a route. The general belief, shared by the directors of Wells Fargo & Company, was that it would be at least ten years before tracks could be laid across the two highest mountain ranges on the continent. Ben Holladay disagreed. Scarcely twenty years before, the Sierra Nevada had been considered impassable to wagons, but thousands had crossed during the gold rush. With California and Oregon growing as they were, and with the Washoe hills yielding silver at the rate of twenty million dollars a year, the West needed railroads in a hurry, and the mountains could no more hold them back than they had held the Forty-Niners.

Ben Holladay had reasoned well. On May 10, 1969 —less than three years from the time he sold out—the Central Pacific and Union Pacific rails were joined at Promontory Point, Utah, and as the golden spike was driven it sounded the death knell of overland stagecoaching. Within another quarter century most of the old trails of the old West would be little more than a memory, buried beneath the cinder beds of the greatest railway system on earth.

Bibliography

ALDRICH, LORENZO D. *A Journal to the Overland Route to California and the Gold Mines*. Dawson's Book Shop, 1950.

ALTROCCHI, JULIA. *The Old California Trail*. Caxton Press, 1945.

BAKELESS, JOHN. *The Eyes of Discovery*. J. B. Lippincott Company, 1950.

BANNING, WM. AND G. H. *Six Horses*. The Century Company, 1930.

BARKER, RUTH L. *Caballeros*. D. Appleton-Century Company, 1931.

BEMIS, SAMUEL F. *Diplomatic History of the United States*. Henry Holt & Company, Inc., 1953.

BERRY, DON. *A Majority of Scoundrels*. Harper & Brothers, 1961.

BILLINGTON, RAY. *Far Western Frontier*. Harper & Brothers, 1956.

BLAKER, ROSEN. *The Golden Conquistadores*. Bobbs-Merrill Company, 1960.

BOLTON, HERBERT E. *Outpost of Empire*. Alfred A. Knopf, Inc., 1931.

BOLTON, HERBERT E. *Padre on Horseback*. Sonora Press, 1932.

BOLTON, HERBERT E. *Rim of Christendom*. The Macmillan Company, 1936.

BROOKS, ELISHA. *A Pioneer Mother of California*. Harr Wagner Publishing Company, 1922.

BRYANT, EDWIN. *What I Saw in California*. Fine Arts Press, 1936.

CALIFORNIA HISTORICAL SOCIETY. *Russians in California*. California Historical Society.

CAUGHEY, JOHN. *History of the Pacific Coast*. John Caughey.

CLELAND, ROBERT. *California Pageant*. Alfred A. Knopf, Inc., 1946.

CLELAND, ROBERT. *From Wilderness to Empire*. Alfred A. Knopf, Inc., 1959.

CLELAND, ROBERT. *Pathfinders*. Powell Publishing Company, 1929.

COMAN, KATHERINE. *Economic Beginnings of the Far West*. The Macmillan Company, 1912.

CONKLING, ROSCOE AND MARGARET. *Butterfield Overland Mail 1857-1869*. Arthur H. Clark Company, 1947.

COOKE, PHILIP ST. G. *Conquest of New Mexico and California*. Bio Books, 1952.

CORLE, EDWIN. *The Gila*. Rinehart & Company, 1951.

CORLE, EDWIN. *The Royal Highway*. Bobbs-Merrill Company, 1949.

COY, OWEN C. *The Great Trek*. Powell Publishing Company, 1931.

DELANO, ALONZO. *Across the Plains and Among the Diggings*. Wilson-Erickson, Inc., 1936.

DELLENBAUGH, F. *Breaking the Wilderness*. G. P. Putnam's Son's, 1905.

DENIS, ALBERTA. *Spanish Alta California*. The Macmillan Company, 1927.

DE VOTO, BERNARD. *The Course of the Empire*. Houghton Mifflin Company, 1952.

DICK, EVERETT. *Vanguards of the Frontier*. Appleton-Century Company, Inc., 1941.

DILLON, R. *California Trail Herd*. Talisman Press, 1961.

DRIGGS, HOWARD. *Westward America*. G. P. Putnam's Sons, 1942.

DUFFUS, R. L. *Santa Fe Trail*. Longmans, Green & Company, 1930.

DUNBAR, SEYMOUR. *A History of Travel*. Bobbs-Merrill Company, 1915.

ECCLESTON, ROBERT. *Overland to California on the Southwest Trail in America*. University of California Press, 1950.

ELDRIDGE, ZOETH. *March of Portola—Discovery of S. F. Bay*. California Promotion Committee, 1909.

ENGLEBERT, OMAR. *Last of the Conquistadors*. Harcourt, Brace & Company, Inc., 1956.

FERGUSSON, ERNA. *New Mexico*. Alfred A. Knopf, Inc., 1951.

FERGUSSON, ERNA. *Our Southwest*. Alfred A. Knopf, Inc., 1952.

FOREMAN, GRANT. *Marcy and the Gold Seekers*. University of Oklahoma Press, 1939.

FOREMAN, GRANT. *Pathfinder in the Southwest*. Arthur H. Clark Company, 1926.

FULLER, GEORGE W. *History of the Pacific Northwest*. Alfred A. Knopf, Inc., 1931.

GARDINER, DOROTHY. *West of the River*. Thomas Y. Crowell Company, 1941.

GARRARD, LEWIS. *Wah-to-Yah and the Taos Trail*. University of Oklahoma Press, 1955.

GEIGER, VINCENT, AND BRYARLY, WAKEMAN. *Trail to California*. Yale University Press, 1959.

GHENT, WM. J. *Early Far West*. Longmans, Green & Company, 1931.

GOETSMANN, WM. *Army Exploration in American West 1803-63*. Yale University Press, 1959.

GOLDER, F. A. *March of the Mormon Battalion*. The Century Co., 1928.

GRIFFIN, J. S. *A Doctor Comes to California*. California Historical Society, 1943.

HAFEN, LEROY AND ANN. *The Old Spanish Trail*. Arthur H. Clark Company, 1955.

HAINES, FRANCIS. *Nez Perce*. University of Oklahoma Press, 1955.

HANCOCK, SAMUEL. *Narrative of Samuel Hancock*. Robert M. McBride & Company, 1927.

HARLOW, ALVIN. *Old Waybills*. The Century Company, 1934.

HARRIS, BENJAMIN. *Gila Trail*. University of Oklahoma Press, 1960.

HENRY, R. S. *Story of the Mexican War*. Bobbs-Merrill Company, 1950.

HOLBROOK, STEWART. *The Columbia*. Rinehart & Company, 1956.

HOLBROOK, STEWART. *Yankee Exodus*. The Macmillan Company, 1950.

HOLLON, W. EUGENE. *Great Days of Overland Stage*. American Heritage, VIII-6, 1957.

HOLLON, W. EUGENE. *Southwest—Old and New*. Alfred A. Knopf, Inc., 1961.

HORGAN, PAUL. *Great River*. Rinehart & Company, 1954.

JACOBS, MELVIN. *Winning Oregon*. Caxton Press, 1938.

JOHANSEN, DOROTHY O., AND GATES, CHARLES M. *Empire of the Columbia*. Harper & Brothers, 1957.

JOHNSTON, WM. G. *Overland to California*. Biobooks, 1948.

KELLER, GEORGE. *A Trip Across the Plains*. Biobooks, 1955.

LAUT, AGNES. *Overland Trail*. Frederick A. Stokes Co., 1929.

LAUT, AGNES. *Pilgrims on the Santa Fe*. Frederick A. Stokes Co., 1931.

LAVENDER, DAVID. *Bent's Fort*. Doubleday & Company, Inc., 1954.

LAVENDER, DAVID. *Land of Giants*. Doubleday & Company, Inc., 1958.

LIENHARD, HEINRICH. *From St. Louis to Sutter's Fort, 1846*. University of Oklahoma Press, 1961.

LOCKWOOD, FRANK C. *Pioneer Days in Arizona*. The Macmillan Company, 1932.

LUCIA, ELLIS. *Saga of Ben Holladay*. Hastings House Publishers, Inc., 1959.

LUMMIS, CHARLES F. *The Spanish Pioneers*. A. C. McClurg & Co., 1929.

MAYNARD, THEODORE. *The Long Road of Father Serra*. Appleton-Century-Crofts, Inc., 1954.

MONAGHAN, JAY. *The Overland Trail*. Bobbs-Merrill Company, 1947.

MORA, JO. *Californios*. Doubleday & Company, Inc., 1949.

MULDER AND MORTENSEN. *Among the Mormons*. Alfred A. Knopf, Inc., 1958.

MURPHY, BILL. *Pictorial History of California*. Fearon Publishers, 1958.

OGDEN, ADELE. *California Sea Otter Trade*. University of California Press, 1941.

OLDER, MRS. FREMONT. *California Missions and Their Romances*. Coward-McCann, Inc., 1938.

PADEN, IRENE. *Wake of the Prairie Schooner.* The Macmillan Company, 1943.

PARRISH, PHILIP H. *Before the Covered Wagon.* Metropolitan Press, 1931.

PATTIE, JAMES OHIO. *The Personal Narrative of James Ohio Pattie.* J. B. Lippincott Company, 1962.

PATTON, ANNALEONE D. *California Mormons.* Deseret Book Co., 1961.

PEATTIE, D. C. *Forward the Nation.* G. P. Putnam's Sons, 1942.

PERRIGO, LYNN I. *Our Spanish Southwest.* Banks, Upshaw & Co., 1960.

PHILLIPS, PAUL. *The Fur Trade.* University of Oklahoma Press, 1961.

RIEGEL, R. E. *America Moves West.* Henry Holt & Company, 1930.

SABIN, E. L. *Kit Carson Days.* Press of the Pioneers, Inc., 1935.

SANDOZ, MARI. *Love Song to the Plains.* Harper & Brothers, 1961.

SCHALLENBERGER, MOSES. *The Opening of the California Trail.* University of California Press, 1953.

STEWART, GEORGE. *Ordeal by Hunger.* Henry Holt & Company, Inc., 1936.

STONE, IRVING. *Immortal Wife.* Doubleday & Company, Inc., 1944.

STONE, IRVING. *Men to Match My Mountains.* Doubleday & Company, Inc., 1956.

TERRELL, JOHN U. *Journey into Darkness.* William Morrow & Company, Inc., 1962.

THOMPSON, R. A. *Fort Ross.* Biobooks, 1951.

VESTAL, STANLEY. *Old Santa Fe Trail.* Houghton Mifflin Company, 1939.

WARE, JOSEPH E. *Emigrant's Guide to California.* Princeton University Press, 1932.

WARREN, SIDNEY. *Farthest Frontier.* The Macmillan Company, 1949.

WATERS, FRANK. *The Colorado.* Rinehart & Company, Inc., 1946.

WELLMAN, PAUL. *Glory, God and Gold.* Doubleday & Company, Inc., 1954.

WILSON, RUFUS R. *Out of the West.* Press of the Pioneers, Inc., 1933.

WINTHER, OSCAR. *The Great Northwest.* Alfred A. Knopf, Inc., 1950.

WINTHER, OSCAR. *The Old Oregon Country.* Stanford University Press, 1950.

WISTAR, I. J. *Autobiography of Gen. Isaac J. Wistar.* Harper & Brothers, 1938.

WYMAN, W. D. *California Emigrant Letters.* Bookman Associates, Inc., 1952.

Index

Adams, John Quincy, 23
Alaska, 58, 61
Allande, Pedro Maria de, 15
Allegheny River, 6
American Board of Foreign Missions, 90, 94
American Philosophical Society, 64
American River, 112
animal trails, 3-4, 5
Apache Indians, 42
Apache Pass, 52
Arapaho Indians, 39, 42, 45, 55
Archuleta, Diego, 52-54
Argonauts, the, 56, 120-123
Arikara village, 71
Arizona, 1
Arkansas River, 6, 12, 14-16, 19, 28-29, 33, 57
Armijo, Antonio, 47, 50-52
Army of the West, 48-53, 120
Ashley, William, 30, 78, 79, 80, 82, 91
Astor, John Jacob, 69, 74-75, 77
Austin, Nevada, 123

Baird, James, 13, 21
Baker, Ore., 74
Bakersfield, Calif., 102
Ball, John, 84

Battle Mountain, Nevada, 103
Bear River, 76, 77, 81, 86, 95, 104
beaver trappers, *see* trappers
Becknell, William, 16-20, 25, 30, 33, 39, 57
Bent, Charles, 54-55
Bent, William, 30, 34-35, 38, 41-48, 55
Benton, Randolph, 96, 97
Benton, Thomas Hart, 23, 29, 96, 98, 104, 105
Bent's Fort, 42-48, 50, 51, 55, 57
Bidwell, John, 102, 103-104
Big Horn River, 78
Big Medicine Trail (*see also* Oregon Trail), 4-5, 58-81
Big Sandy River, 95
Bishop's Creek, 102
Bismarck, N.D., 65
Blackfoot Indians, 68-69, 71-72, 78
Boise, Idaho, 75
Boise Basin, 93
Boit, John, 62-63, 70
Bonneville, Benjamin, 100
Bridger, Jim, 30, 78, 81, 117
Bridger's Fort, *see* Fort Bridger
Brown, James, 121, 122

139